THE BIG
BOOK OF
MENSA
PUZZLES

THIS IS A CARLTON BOOK

CLD 20678

This edition published in 1997 for Colour Library Direct,
Godalming Business Centre,
Woolsack Way, Godalming,
Surrey GU7 1XW

10 9 8 7 6 5 4 3 2 1

Text and puzzle content copyright © Mensa Limited 1995, 1997
Design and artwork copyright © Carlton Books Limited 1995, 1997

A CIP catalogue for this book is available from the British Library

ISBN 1-85833-811-5

Designed by Jacqui Ellis

Printed and bound in Great Britain

THE BIG BOOK OF MENSA PUZZLES

HAROLD GALE

Colour Library Direct

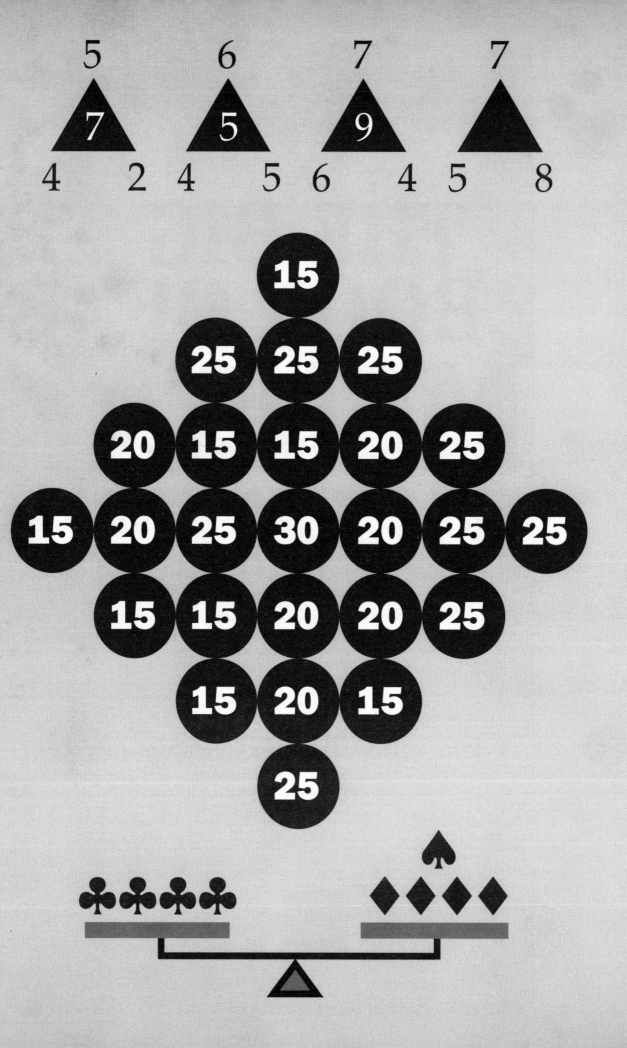

INTRODUCTION TO NUMBER PUZZLES

Puzzles using numbers have become more and more popular over the years. Some of the puzzles are purely mathematical and involve the use of simple processes. There are others, however, which although appearing to use one branch of mathematics, can be solved more easily and quickly using a little logical thought. Before attempting a puzzle it should be considered very carefully and quite often the solution stands out clearly.

One main aid in the production of number puzzles is the computer. Once a programme has been written puzzles can be generated at a very fast rate. However this does not dispense with the need for other human assistance.

I have an extremely able helper in Carolyn Skitt. She checks, criticizes and improves on many of the puzzles produced. Without Carolyn this book would still be in the making. Help has also come from other quarters. Joanne Harris spent a great deal of time perfecting the tinted puzzles, Bobby Raikhy worked on the many diagrammatic styles, and David Ballheimer checked the proofs. But what of Mensa?

If you can solve the puzzles can you join the organization? You should have no problem. These are fun puzzles but by no means easy. If you can work these out, the Mensa test should prove to be no hurdle and you should easily qualify. Once you have joined, you will find a feeling of satisfaction that very few experience in a lifetime. You will meet people of all walks of life but of similar brain power. A scientist can meet a poet; a composer, an architect. The broadening of intellectual vision is amazing. The new horizon is formidable, but challenging. I invite you to join this ever-expanding group of people, where race, religion or political persuasion are not blocks but keys: keys to opening new doors of understanding, friendship and considered discussion.

There are 40,000 Mensa members in the British Isles alone. There are over 50,000 in the USA. There are 120,000 throughout the world. Write to Mensa, Mensa House, St John's Square, Wolverhampton WV2 1AH, England, or American Mensa Limited at 2626 E 14th Street, Brooklyn, New York 11235-3992, USA.

Harold Gale
Former Executive Director of British Mensa
March,1993

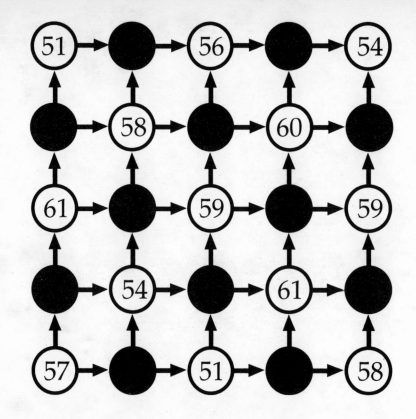

NUMBER PUZZLE 1

Move from the bottom left-hand corner to the top right-hand
corner following the arrows. Add the numbers on your route
together. If each black spot is worth minus 23,
how many different routes are there to score 188?

ANSWER 62

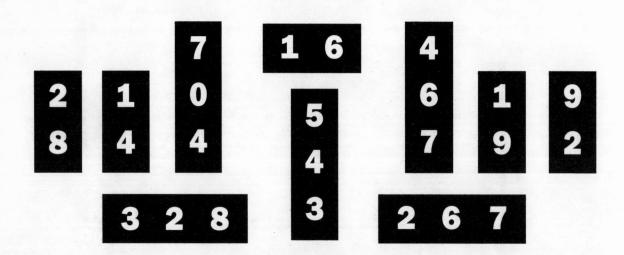

NUMBER PUZZLE 2

Place the tiles in a square to give some five-figure numbers.
When this has been done accurately the same
five numbers can be read both down and across.
How does the finished square look?

ANSWER 10

NUMBER PUZZLE 3

Start in the middle circle and move from circle to touching circle.
Collect the four numbers which will total 70. Once a route has
been found return to the middle circle and start again.
If a route can be found, which obeys the above rules but follows
both a clockwise and an anticlockwise path, it is treated as two
different routes.
How many different ways are there?

ANSWER 103

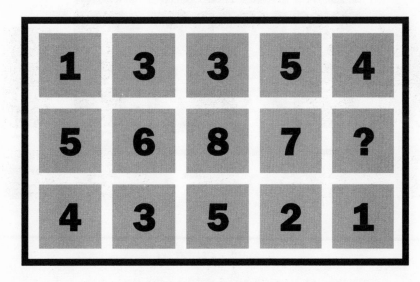

NUMBER PUZZLE 4

Which number should replace the question mark in the diagram?

ANSWER 51

You have four shots with each go to score 75. Aim at this target and work out how many different ways there are to make the score. Assume each shot scores and once four numbers have been used the same four cannot be used again in another order.
How many are there?

ANSWER 92

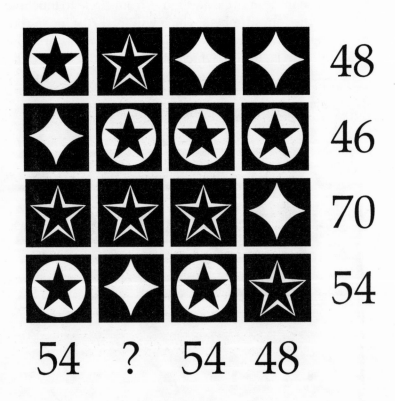

NUMBER PUZZLE 6

The contents of each box has a value. The total of the values is shown alongside a row or beneath a column. Which number should replace the question mark?

ANSWER 40

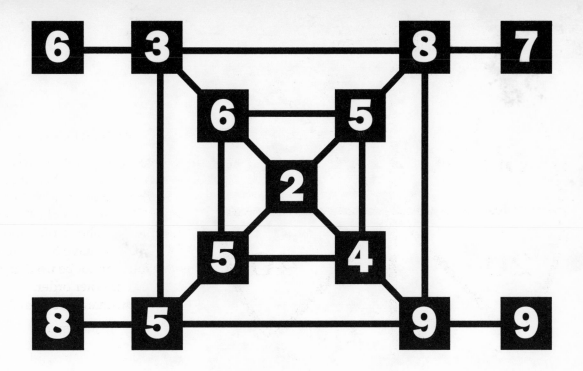

NUMBER PUZZLE 7

Start at any corner number and collect another four numbers by
following the paths shown. Add the five numbers together.
What is the highest total which can be attained?

ANSWER 82

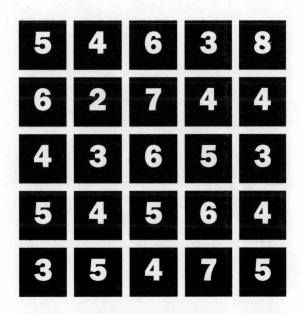

NUMBER PUZZLE 8

Move from square to adjacent square either vertically or horizontally. Begin at the bottom left-hand square and end at the top right-
hand square. Collect nine numbers and total them. How many
different ways are there to total 38?

ANSWER 30

A B C D E

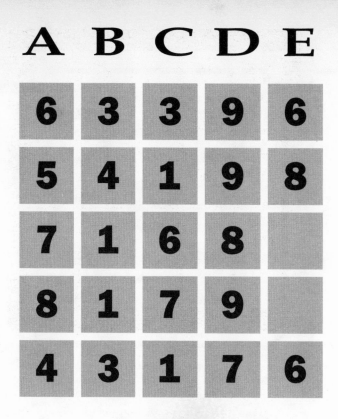

A	B	C	D	E
6	3	3	9	6
5	4	1	9	8
7	1	6	8	
8	1	7	9	
4	3	1	7	6

NUMBER PUZZLE 9

There is a relationship between the columns of numbers in this diagram. The letters above the grid are there to help you. Which number should be placed in the empty squares?

ANSWER 72

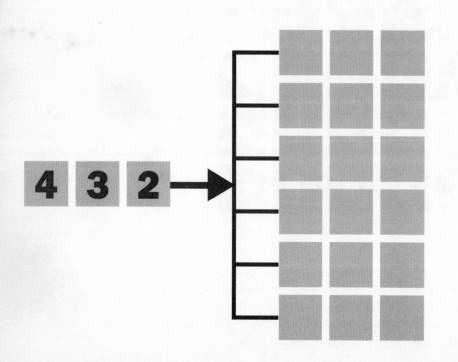

NUMBER PUZZLE 10

Place six three digit numbers of 100 plus at the end of 432 so that six numbers of six digits are produced. When each number is divided by 151 six whole numbers can be found. Which numbers should be placed in the grid?

ANSWER 20

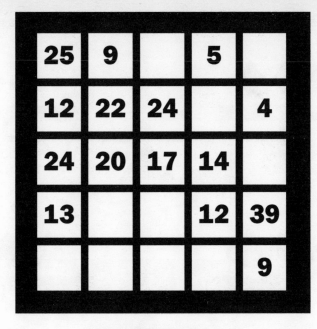

NUMBER PUZZLE 11

Each row, column and five-figure diagonal line
in this diagram must total 85. Four different numbers must be
used, as many times as necessary, to achieve this.
What are the numbers?

ANSWER 61

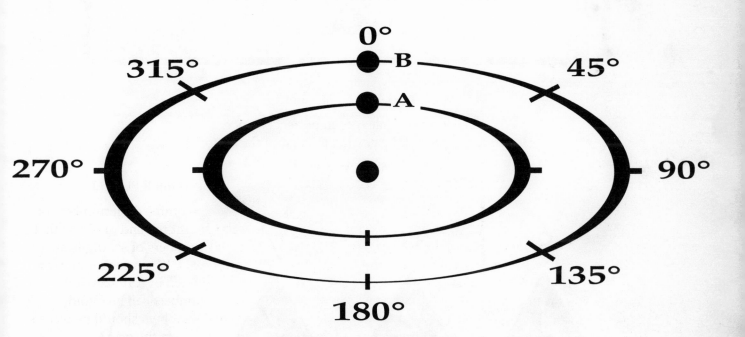

NUMBER PUZZLE 12

Two planets are in line with each other and the sun.
The outer planet will orbit the sun every twelve years. The inner
planet takes three years. Both move in a clockwise direction.
When will they next form a straight line with each other and the
sun? The diagram should help you.

ANSWER 9

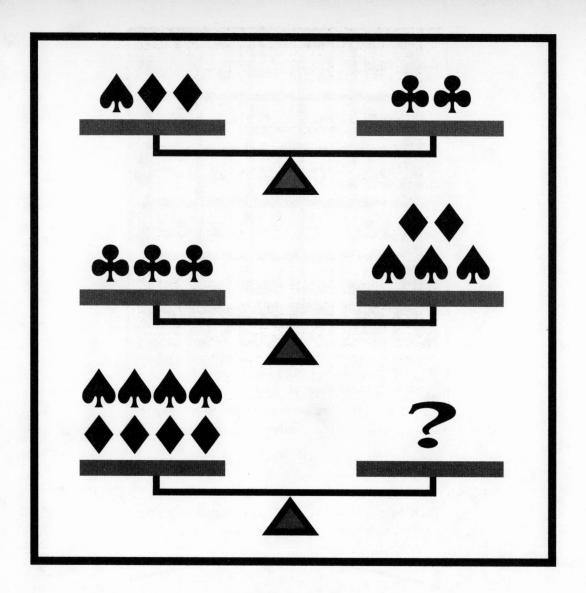

NUMBER PUZZLE 13

The top two scales are in perfect balance.
How many clubs will be needed to balance the bottom set?

ANSWER 102

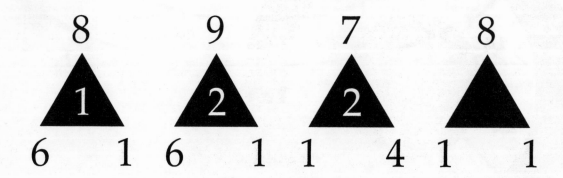

NUMBER PUZZLE 14

Which figure should be placed in the empty triangle?

ANSWER 50

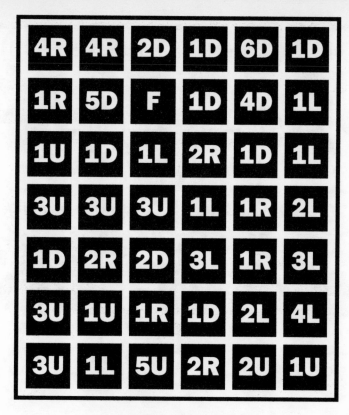

4R	4R	2D	1D	6D	1D
1R	5D	F	1D	4D	1L
1U	1D	1L	2R	1D	1L
3U	3U	3U	1L	1R	2L
1D	2R	2D	3L	1R	3L
3U	1U	1R	1D	2L	4L
3U	1L	5U	2R	2U	1U

NUMBER PUZZLE 15

Here is an unusual safe. Each of the buttons must be pressed once
only in the correct order to open it. The last button is always
marked F. The number of moves and the direction is marked on
each button. Thus 1U would mean one move up
whilst 1L would mean one move to the left.
Which button is the first you must press?

ANSWER 91

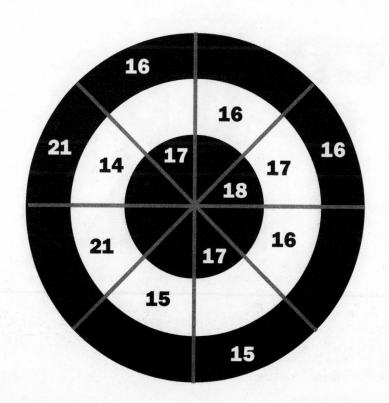

NUMBER PUZZLE 16

Complete the grid in such a way
that each segment of three numbers
totals the same.
When this has been done correctly
each of the three concentric circles of
eight numbers will produce three
identical totals.
Now complete the diagram.

ANSWER 39

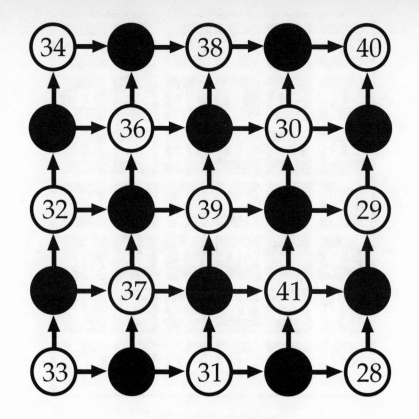

NUMBER PUZZLE 17

Move from the bottom left-hand corner to the top right-hand
corner following the arrows. Add the numbers on your route
together. If each black spot is worth minus 8,
how many different routes are there to score 155?

ANSWER 81

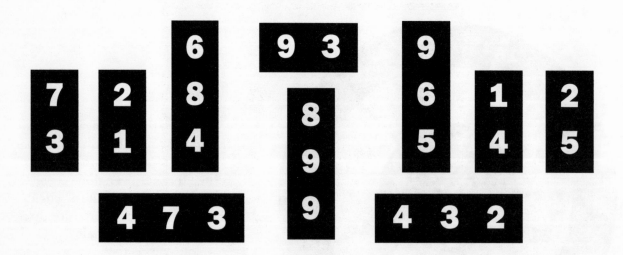

NUMBER PUZZLE 18

Place the tiles in a square to give some five-figure numbers. When
this has been done accurately the same
five numbers can be read both down and across.
How does the finished square look?

ANSWER 29

NUMBER PUZZLE 19

Start in the middle circle and move from circle to touching circle.
Collect the four numbers which will total 86. Once a route has
been found return to the middle circle and start again.
If a route can be found, which obeys the above rules but follows
both a clockwise and an anti-clockwise path, it is treated as two
different routes. How many different ways are there?

ANSWER 71

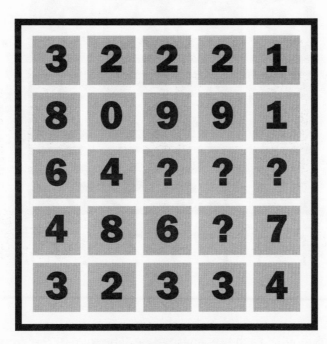

NUMBER PUZZLE 20

Which number should replace the question marks in the diagram?

ANSWER 19

NUMBER PUZZLE 21

You have four shots with each go to score 51. Aim at this target and work out how many different ways there are to make the score. Assume each shot scores and once four numbers have been used the same four cannot be used again in another order.
How many are there?

ANSWER 8

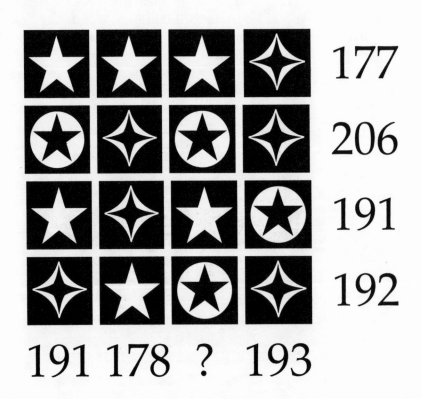

191 178 ? 193

NUMBER PUZZLE 22

The contents of each box has a value. The total of the values is shown alongside a row or beneath a column. Which number should replace the question mark?

ANSWER 60

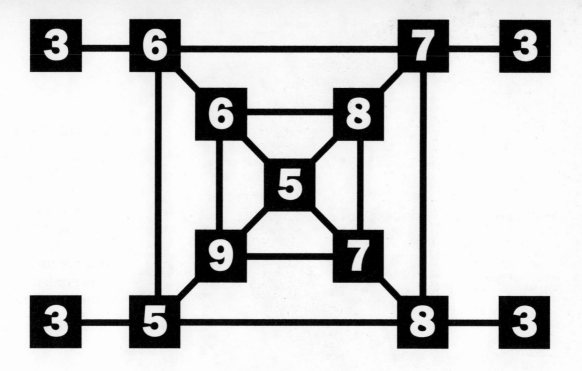

NUMBER PUZZLE 23

Start at any corner number and collect another four numbers by following the paths shown. Add the five numbers together. How many times can you score 27?

ANSWER 101

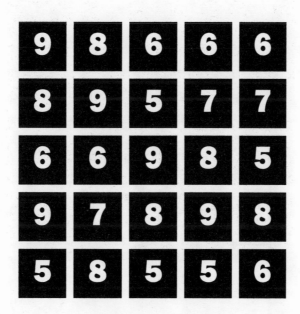

NUMBER PUZZLE 24

Move from square to adjacent square either vertically or horizontally. Begin at the bottom left-hand square and end at the top right-hand square. Collect nine numbers and total them. How many different ways are there to total 66?

ANSWER 49

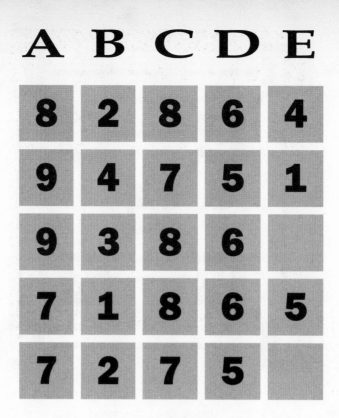

A B C D E

A	B	C	D	E
8	2	8	6	4
9	4	7	5	1
9	3	8	6	
7	1	8	6	5
7	2	7	5	

NUMBER PUZZLE 25

There is a relationship between the columns of numbers in this diagram. The letters above the grid are there to help you. Which number should be placed in the empty squares?

ANSWER 90

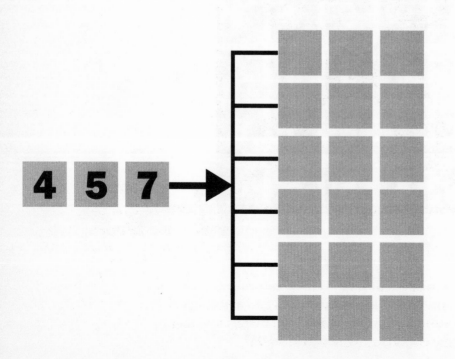

NUMBER PUZZLE 26

Place six three digit numbers of 100 plus at the end of 457 so that six numbers of six digits are produced. When each number is divided by 55.5 six whole numbers can be found. Which numbers should be placed in the grid?

ANSWER 38

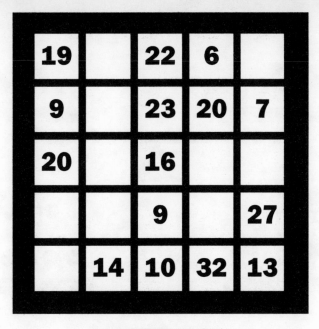

NUMBER PUZZLE 27

Each row, column and five-figure diagonal line
in this diagram must total 80. Three different numbers must be
used, as many times as necessary, to achieve this.
What are the numbers?

ANSWER 80

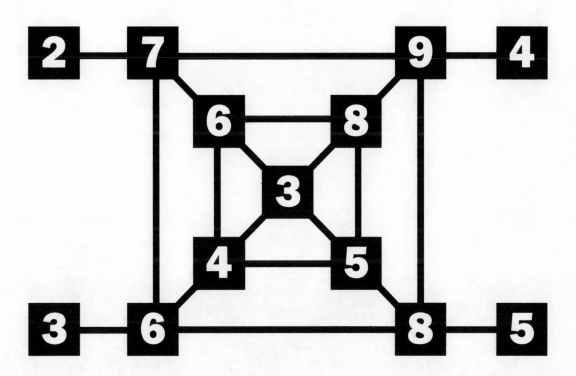

NUMBER PUZZLE 28

Start at the corner number and collect another four numbers by
following the paths shown. Add the five numbers together.
How many times can you score 24?

ANSWER 28

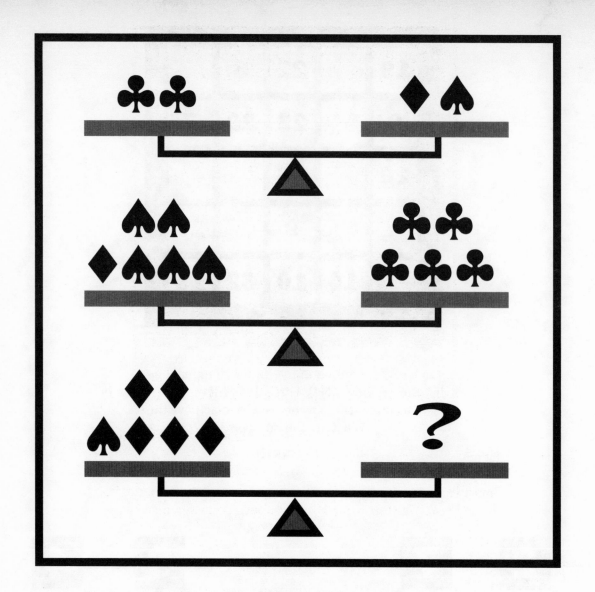

NUMBER PUZZLE 29

The top two scales are in perfect balance.
How many clubs will be needed to balance the bottom set?

ANSWER 70

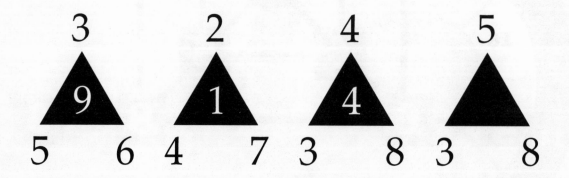

NUMBER PUZZLE 30

Which figure should be placed in the empty triangle?

ANSWER 18

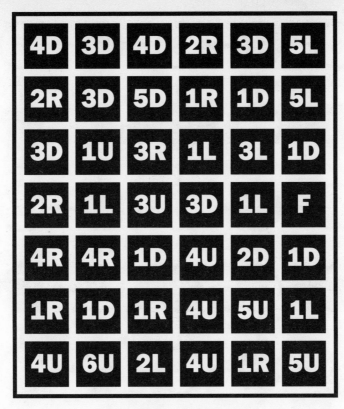

4D	3D	4D	2R	3D	5L
2R	3D	5D	1R	1D	5L
3D	1U	3R	1L	3L	1D
2R	1L	3U	3D	1L	F
4R	4R	1D	4U	2D	1D
1R	1D	1R	4U	5U	1L
4U	6U	2L	4U	1R	5U

NUMBER PUZZLE 31

Here is an unusual safe. Each of the buttons must be pressed once
only in the correct order to open it. The last button is always
marked F. The number of moves and the direction is marked on
each button. Thus 1U would mean one move up
whilst 1L would mean one move to the left.
Which button is the first you must press?

ANSWER 59

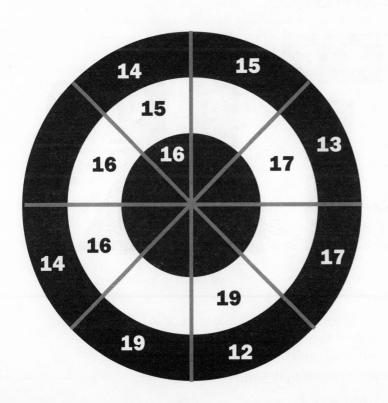

NUMBER PUZZLE 32

Complete the grid in such a way
that each segment of three numbers
totals the same.
When this has been done correctly
each of the three concentric circles of
eight numbers will produce three
identical totals.
Now complete the diagram.

ANSWER 7

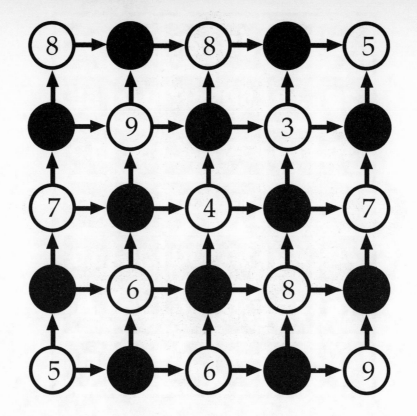

NUMBER PUZZLE 33

Move from the bottom left-hand corner to the top right-hand
corner following the arrows. Add the numbers on your route
together. If each black spot is worth 2,
how many different routes are there to score 40?

ANSWER 100

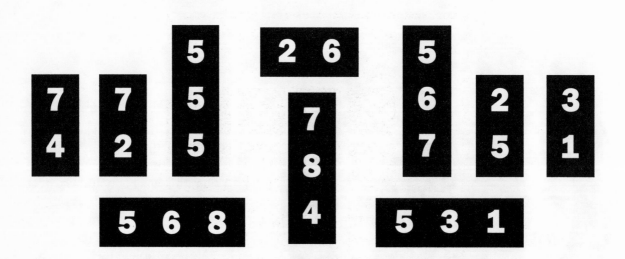

NUMBER PUZZLE 34

Place the tiles in a square to give some five-figure numbers. When
this has been done accurately the same
five numbers can be read both down and across.
How does the finished square look?

ANSWER 48

NUMBER PUZZLE 35

Start in the middle circle and move from circle to touching circle.
Collect the four numbers which will total 90. Once a route has
been found return to the middle circle and start again.
If a route can be found, which obeys the above rules but follows
both a clockwise and an anticlockwise path, it is treated as two
different routes. How many different ways are there?

ANSWER 89

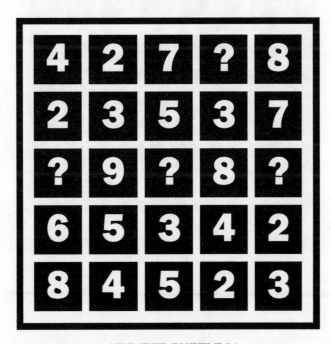

NUMBER PUZZLE 36

Which number should replace the question mark in the diagram?

ANSWER 37

NUMBER PUZZLE 37

You have four shots with each go to score 49. Aim at this target and work out how many different ways there are to make the score. Assume each shot scores and once four numbers have been used the same four cannot be used again in another order.
How many are there?

ANSWER 79

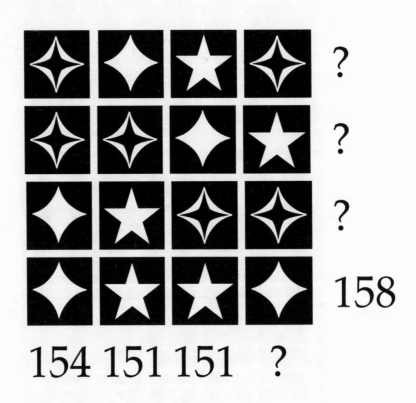

154   151   151   ?

NUMBER PUZZLE 38

The contents of each box has a value. The total of the values is shown alongside a row or beneath a column. Which number should replace the question marks?

ANSWER 27

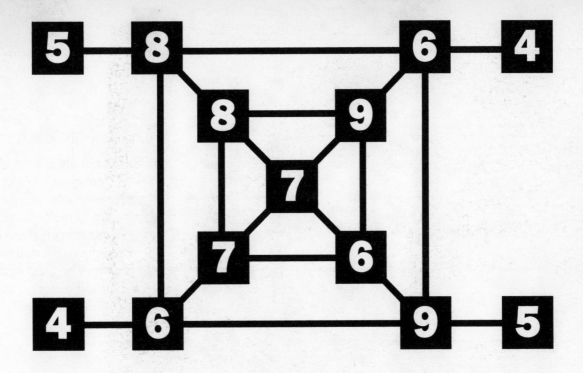

NUMBER PUZZLE 39

Start at the corner number and collect another four numbers by
following the paths shown. Add the five numbers together.
What is the lowest number you can score?

ANSWER 69

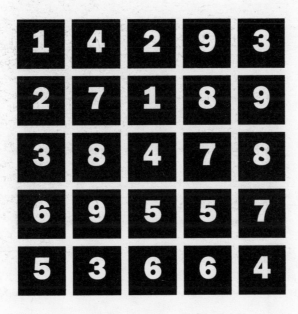

NUMBER PUZZLE 40

Move from square to adjacent square either vertically or horizontally. Begin at the bottom left-hand square and end at the top right-
hand square. Collect nine numbers and total them.
How many different ways are there to total 35?

ANSWER 17

A B C D E

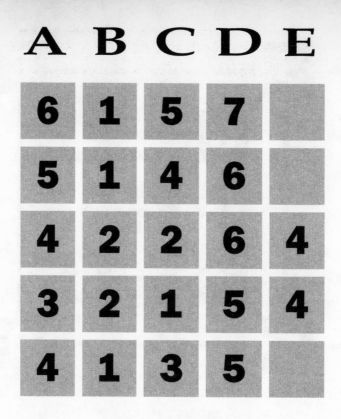

A	B	C	D	E
6	1	5	7	
5	1	4	6	
4	2	2	6	4
3	2	1	5	4
4	1	3	5	

NUMBER PUZZLE 41

There is a relationship between the columns of numbers in this diagram. The letters above the grid are there to help you. Which number should be placed in the empty squares?

ANSWER 58

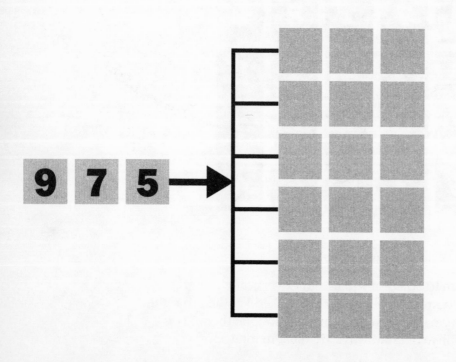

NUMBER PUZZLE 42

Place six three digit numbers of 100 plus at the end of 975 so that six numbers of six digits are produced. When each number is divided by 65.5 six whole numbers can be found. Which numbers should be placed in the grid?

ANSWER 6

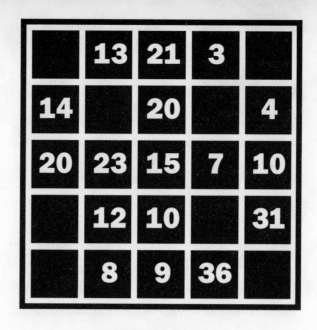

NUMBER PUZZLE 43

Each row, column and five-figure diagonal line
in this diagram must total 75. Three different numbers must be
used, as many times as necessary, to achieve this.
What are the numbers?

ANSWER 99

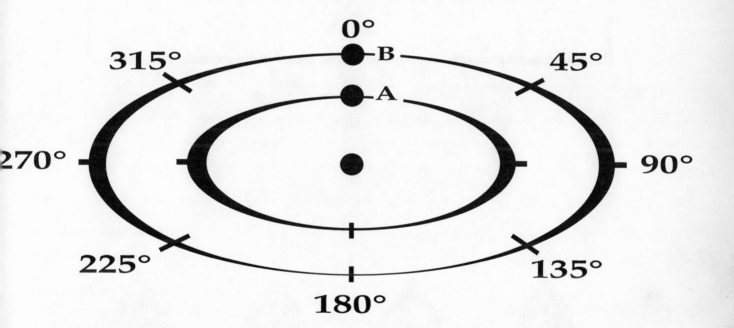

NUMBER PUZZLE 44

Two planets are in line with each other and the sun.
The outer planet will orbit the sun every six years. The inner
planet takes two years. Both move in a clockwise direction. When
will they next form a straight line with each other and the sun?
The diagram should help you.

ANSWER 47

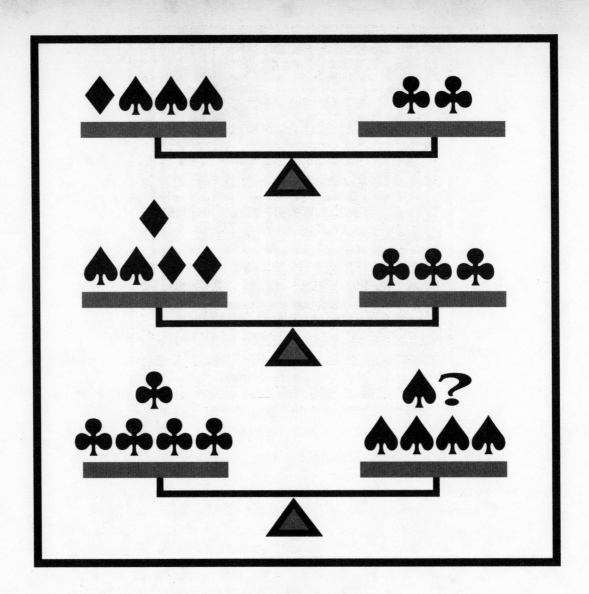

NUMBER PUZZLE 45

The top two scales are in perfect balance.
How many diamonds will be needed to balance the bottom set?

ANSWER 88

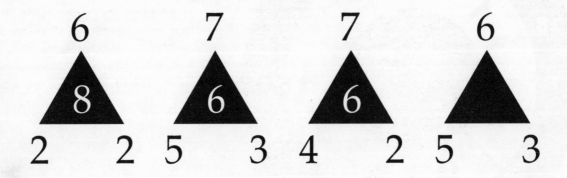

NUMBER PUZZLE 46

Which figure should be placed in the empty triangle?

ANSWER 36

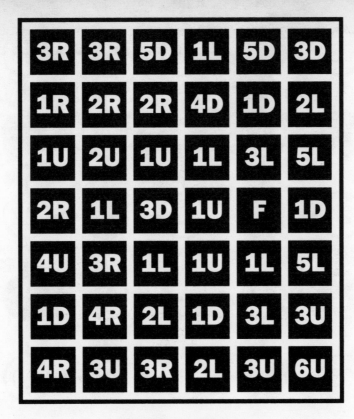

NUMBER PUZZLE 47

Here is an unusual safe. Each of the buttons bar one must be pressed once only in the correct order to open it. The last button is always marked F. The number of moves and the direction is marked on each button. Thus 1U would mean one move up whilst 1L would mean one move to the left.
Which button is the first you must press?

ANSWER 78

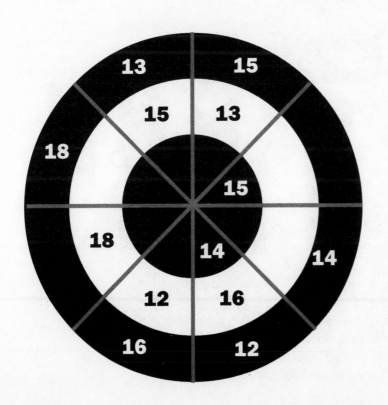

NUMBER PUZZLE 48

Complete the grid in such a way that each segment of three numbers totals the same.
When this has been done correctly each of the three concentric circles of eight numbers will produce identical totals.
Now complete the diagram.

ANSWER 26

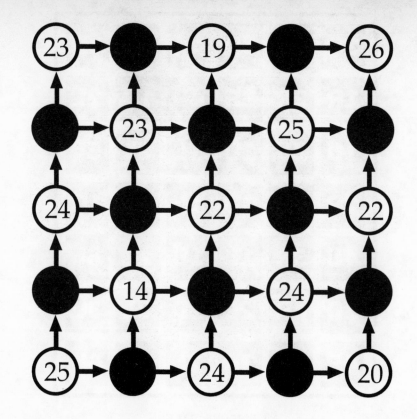

NUMBER PUZZLE 49

Move from the bottom left-hand corner to the top right-hand
corner following the arrows. Add the numbers on your route
together. If each black spot is worth minus 13,
how many different routes are there to score 69?

ANSWER 68

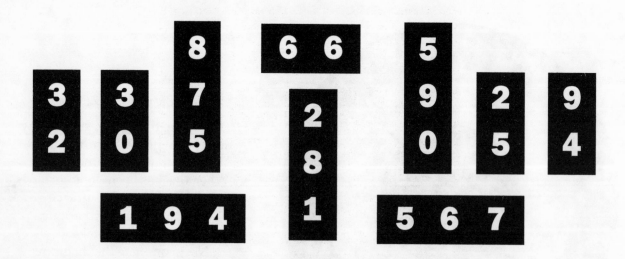

NUMBER PUZZLE 50

Place the tiles in a square to give some five-figure numbers. When
this has been done accurately the same
five numbers can be read both down and across.
How does the finished square look?

ANSWER 16

NUMBER PUZZLE 51

Start in the middle circle and move from circle to touching circle.
Collect the four numbers which will total 42. Once a route has
been found return to the middle circle and start again.
If a route can be found, which obeys the above rules but follows
both a clockwise and an anticlockwise path, it is treated as two
different routes. How many different ways are there?

ANSWER 57

NUMBER PUZZLE 52

Which number should replace the question marks in the diagram?

ANSWER 5

NUMBER PUZZLE 53

You have four shots with each go to score 48. Aim at this target and work out how many different ways there are to make the score. Assume each shot scores and once four numbers have been used the same four cannot be used again in another order.
How many are there?

ANSWER 98

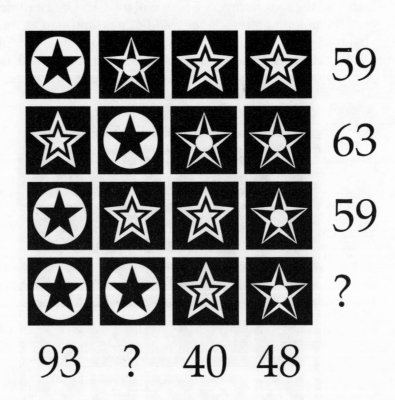

NUMBER PUZZLE 54

The contents of each box has a value. The total of the values is shown alongside a row or beneath a column. Which number should replace the question marks?

ANSWER 46

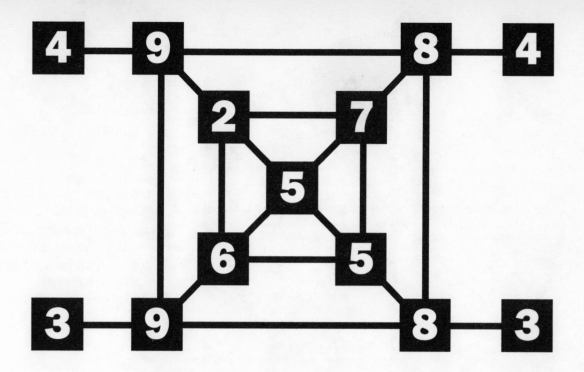

NUMBER PUZZLE 55

Start at any corner number and collect another four numbers by
following the paths shown. Add the five numbers together.
How many times can you score 29?

ANSWER 87

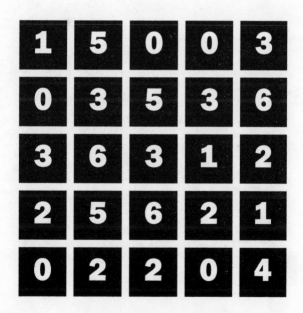

NUMBER PUZZLE 56

Move from square to adjacent square either vertically or
horizontally. Begin at the bottom left-hand square and end at the
top right-hand square. Collect nine numbers and total them.
How many different ways are there to total 30?

ANSWER 35

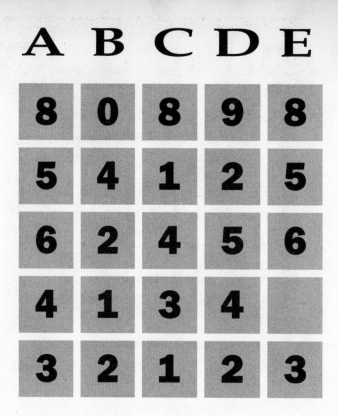

A B C D E

A	B	C	D	E
8	0	8	9	8
5	4	1	2	5
6	2	4	5	6
4	1	3	4	
3	2	1	2	3

NUMBER PUZZLE 57

There is a relationship between the columns of numbers in this diagram. The letters above the grid are there to help you. Which number should be placed in the empty squares?

ANSWER 77

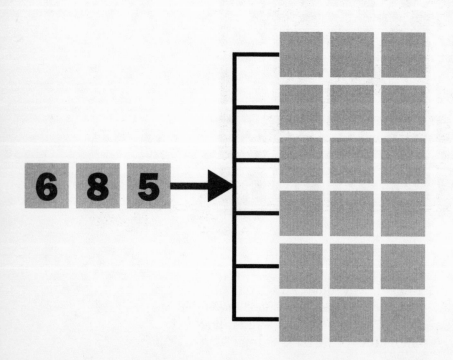

6 8 5

NUMBER PUZZLE 58

Place six three digit numbers of 100 plus at the end of 685 so that six numbers of six digits are produced. When each number is divided by 111 six whole numbers can be found. Which numbers should be placed in the grid?

ANSWER 25

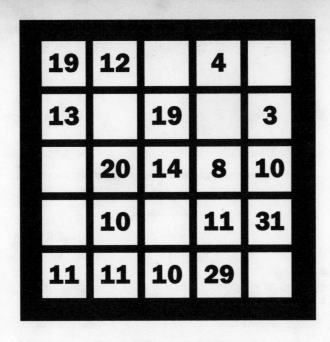

NUMBER PUZZLE 59

Each row, column and five-figure diagonal line
in this diagram must total 70. Three different numbers must be
used, as many times as necessary, to achieve this.
What are the numbers?

ANSWER 67

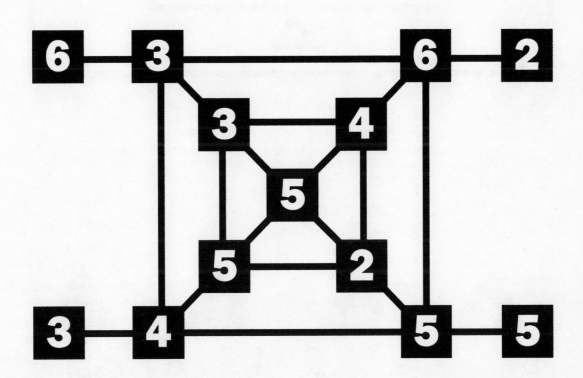

NUMBER PUZZLE 60

Start at the corner number and collect another four numbers by
following the paths shown. Add the five numbers together.
How many times can you score 17?

ANSWER 15

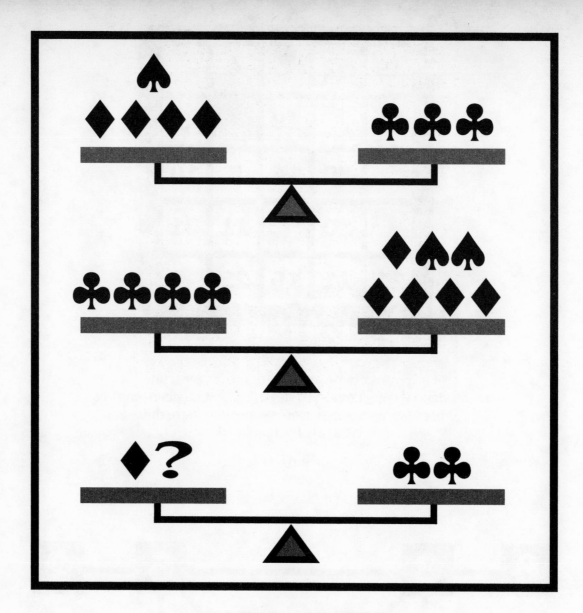

NUMBER PUZZLE 61

The top two scales are in perfect balance.
How many spades will be needed to balance the bottom set?

ANSWER 56

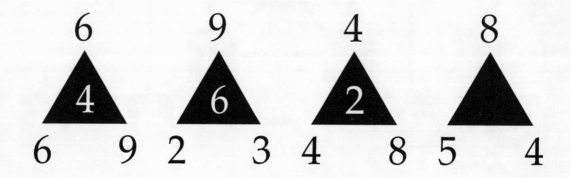

NUMBER PUZZLE 62

Which figure should be placed in the empty triangle?

ANSWER 4

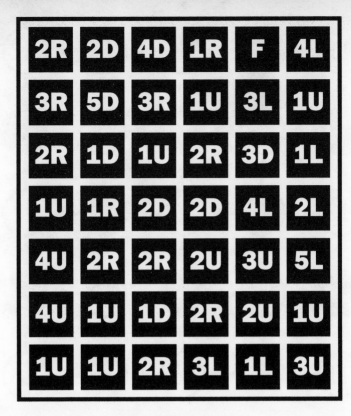

2R	2D	4D	1R	F	4L
3R	5D	3R	1U	3L	1U
2R	1D	1U	2R	3D	1L
1U	1R	2D	2D	4L	2L
4U	2R	2R	2U	3U	5L
4U	1U	1D	2R	2U	1U
1U	1U	2R	3L	1L	3U

NUMBER PUZZLE 63

Here is an unusual safe. Each of the buttons must be pressed once
only in the correct order to open it. The last button is always
marked F. The number of moves and the direction is marked on
each button. Thus 1U would mean one move up
whilst 1L would mean one move to the left.
Which button is the first you must press?

ANSWER 97

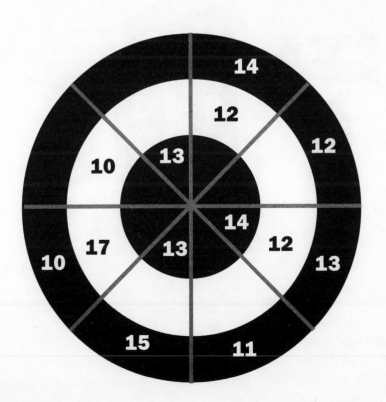

NUMBER PUZZLE 64

Complete the grid in such a way
that each segment of three numbers
totals the same.
When this has been done correctly
each of the three concentric circles of
eight numbers will produce
identical totals.
Now complete the diagram.

ANSWER 45

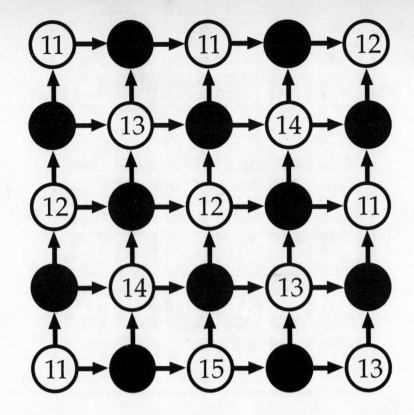

NUMBER PUZZLE 65

Move from the bottom left-hand corner to the top right-hand
corner following the arrows. Add the numbers on your route
together. If each black spot is worth 9,
how many different routes are there to score 94?

ANSWER 86

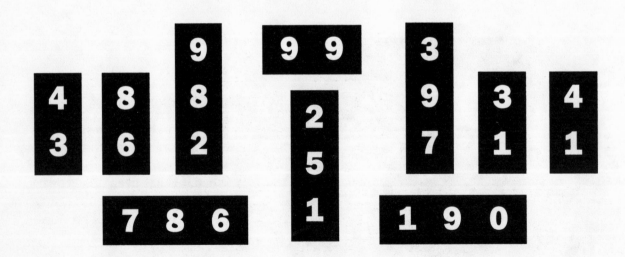

NUMBER PUZZLE 66

Place the tiles in a square to give some five-figure numbers. When
this has been done accurately the same
five numbers can be read both downwards and across.
How does the finished square look?

ANSWER 34

NUMBER PUZZLE 67

Start in the middle circle and move from circle to touching circle.
Collect the four numbers which will total 15. Once a route has
been found return to the middle circle and start again.
If a route can be found, which obeys the above rules but follows
both a clockwise and an anticlockwise path, it is treated as two
different routes. How many different ways are there?

ANSWER 76

NUMBER PUZZLE 68

Which number should replace the question marks in the diagram?

ANSWER 24

NUMBER PUZZLE 69

You have three shots with each go to score 26. Aim at this target and work out how many different ways there are to make the score. Assume each shot scores and once three numbers have been used the same three cannot be used again in another order.
How many are there?

ANSWER 66

84

117

?

?

96 95 106 118

NUMBER PUZZLE 70

The contents of each box has a value. The total of the values is shown alongside a row or beneath a column. Which number should replace the question marks?

ANSWER 14

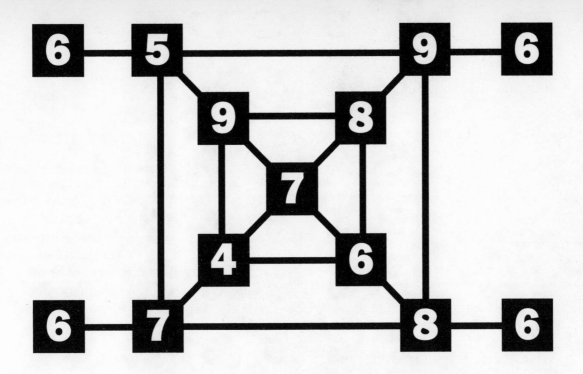

NUMBER PUZZLE 71

Start at any corner number and collect another four numbers by
following the paths shown. Add the five numbers together.
What is the highest number you can score?

ANSWER 55

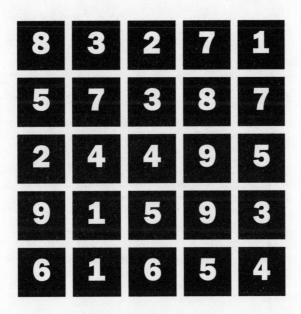

NUMBER PUZZLE 72

Move from square to adjacent square either vertically or horizontally. Begin at the bottom left-hand square and end at the top right-
hand square. Collect nine numbers and total them.
What is the lowest possible score?

ANSWER 3

A B C D E

A	B	C	D	E
9	2	9	7	
5	2	5	3	1
5	1	6	4	3
5	0	7	5	
6	3	5	3	0

NUMBER PUZZLE 73

There is a relationship between the columns of numbers in this diagram. The letters above the grid are there to help you. Which number should be placed in the empty squares?

ANSWER 96

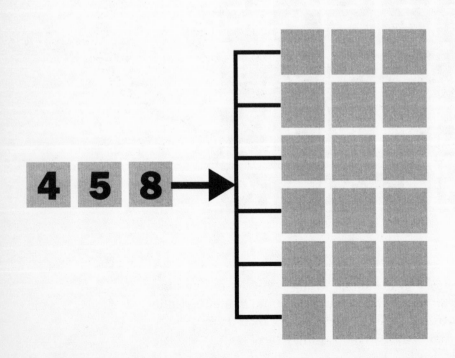

NUMBER PUZZLE 74

Place six three digit numbers of 100 plus at the end of 458 so that six numbers of six digits are produced. When each number is divided by 122 six whole numbers can be found. Which numbers should be placed in the grid?

ANSWER 44

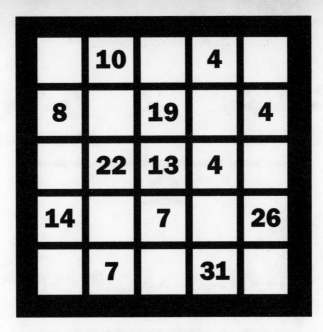

NUMBER PUZZLE 75

Each row, column and five-figure diagonal line
in this diagram must total 65. Two different numbers must be
used, as many times as necessary, to achieve this.
What are the numbers?

ANSWER 85

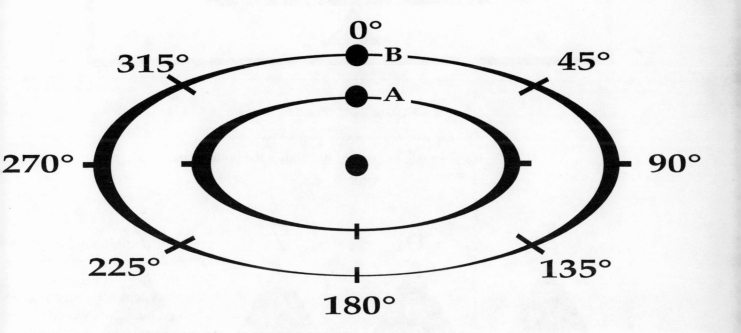

NUMBER PUZZLE 76

Two planets are in line with each other and the sun.
The outer planet will orbit the sun every fifteen years. The inner
planet takes five years. Both move in a clockwise direction. When
will they next form a straight line with each other and the sun?
The diagram should help you.

ANSWER 33

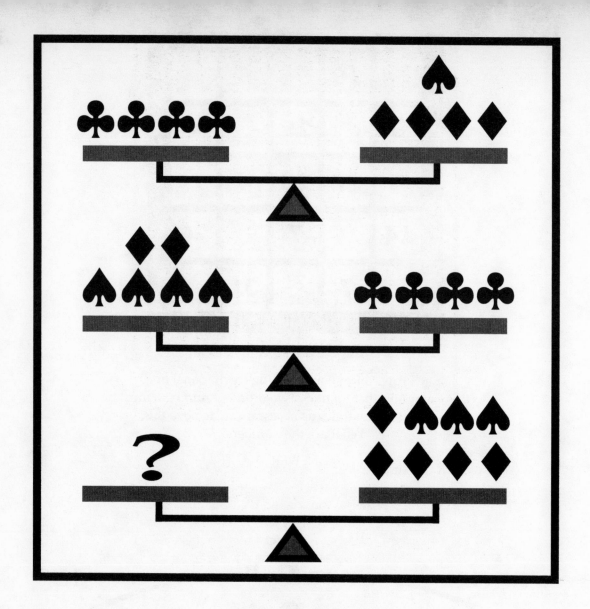

NUMBER PUZZLE 77

The top two scales are in perfect balance.
How many clubs will be needed to balance the bottom set?

ANSWER 75

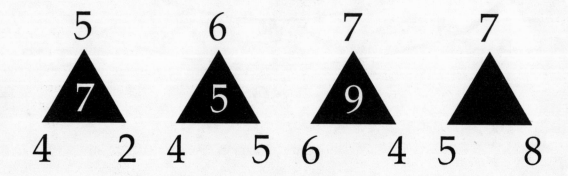

NUMBER PUZZLE 78

Which figure should be placed in the empty triangle?

ANSWER 23

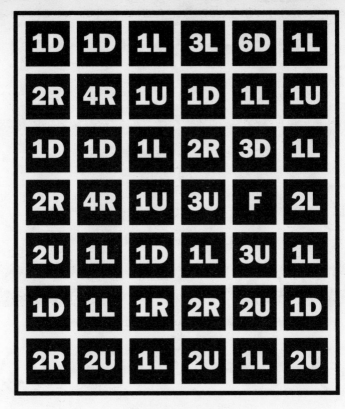

1D	1D	1L	3L	6D	1L
2R	4R	1U	1D	1L	1U
1D	1D	1L	2R	3D	1L
2R	4R	1U	3U	F	2L
2U	1L	1D	1L	3U	1L
1D	1L	1R	2R	2U	1D
2R	2U	1L	2U	1L	2U

NUMBER PUZZLE 79

Here is an unusual safe. Each of the buttons must be pressed once
only in the correct order to open it. The last button is always
marked F. The number of moves and the direction is marked on
each button. Thus 1U would mean one move up
whilst 1L would mean one move to the left.
Which button is the first you must press?

ANSWER 65

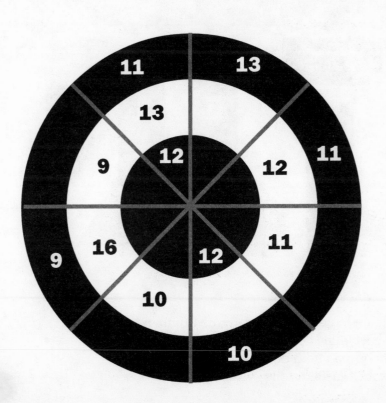

NUMBER PUZZLE 80

Complete the grid in such a way
that each segment of three numbers
totals the same.
When this has been done correctly
each of the three concentric circles of
eight numbers will produce
identical totals.
Now complete the diagram.

ANSWER 13

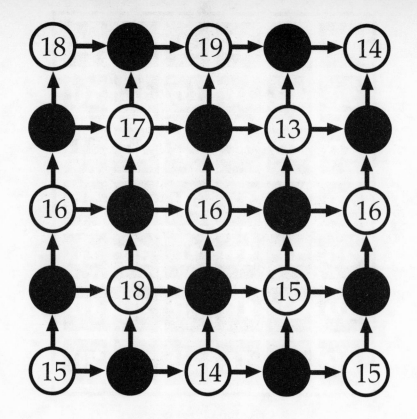

NUMBER PUZZLE 81

Move from the bottom left-hand corner to the top right-hand corner following the arrows. Add the numbers on your route together. If each black spot is worth minus 7, how many different routes are there to score 51?

ANSWER 54

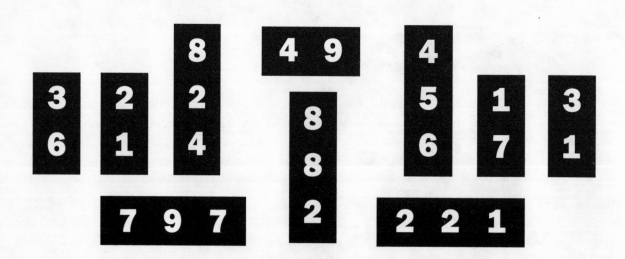

NUMBER PUZZLE 82

Place the tiles in the square to give some five-figure numbers. When this has been done accurately the same five numbers can be read both down and across. How does the finished square look?

ANSWER 2

NUMBER PUZZLE 83

Start in the middle circle and move from circle to touching circle. Collect the four numbers which will total 100. Once a route has been found return to the middle circle and start again.
If a route can be found, which obeys the above rules but follows both a clockwise and an anticlockwise path, it is treated as two different routes.
How many different ways are there?

ANSWER 95

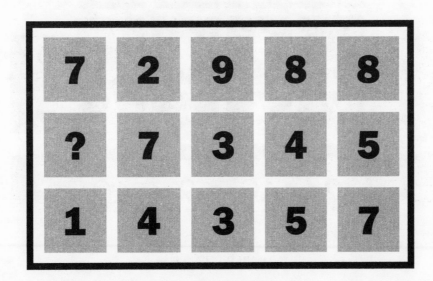

NUMBER PUZZLE 84

Which number should replace the question mark in the diagram?

ANSWER 43

NUMBER PUZZLE 85

You have three shots with each go to score 42. Aim at this target and work out how many different ways there are to make the score. Assume each shot scores and once three numbers have been used the same three cannot be used again in another order.
How many are there?

ANSWER 84

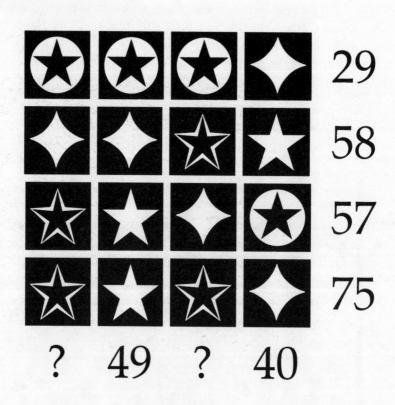

29

58

57

75

? 49 ? 40

NUMBER PUZZLE 86

The contents of each box has a value. The total of the values is shown alongside a row or beneath a column. Which number should replace the question mark?

ANSWER 32

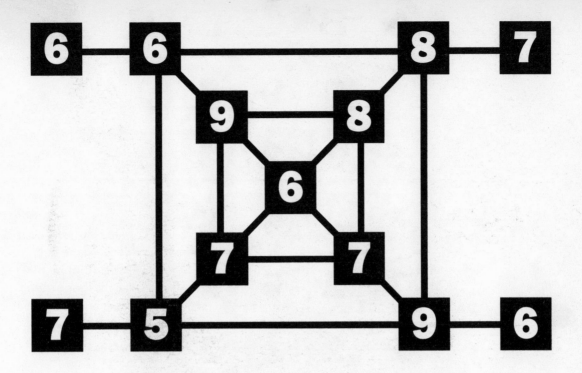

NUMBER PUZZLE 87

Start at any corner number and collect another four numbers by
following the paths shown. Add the five numbers together.
What is the highest number you can score
and how many times can you score it?

ANSWER 74

NUMBER PUZZLE 88

Move from square to adjacent square either vertically or horizontally. Begin at the bottom left-hand square and end at the top right-
hand square. Collect nine numbers and total them.
How many times can you score 60?

ANSWER 22

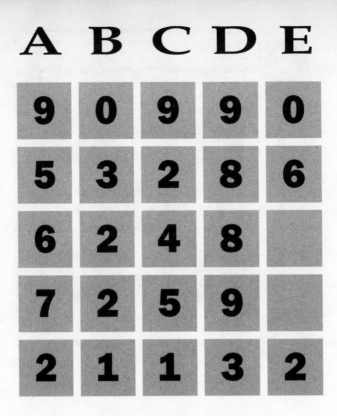

A B C D E

A	B	C	D	E
9	0	9	9	0
5	3	2	8	6
6	2	4	8	
7	2	5	9	
2	1	1	3	2

NUMBER PUZZLE 89

There is a relationship between the columns of numbers in this diagram. The letters above the grid are there to help you. Which number should be placed in the empty squares?

ANSWER 64

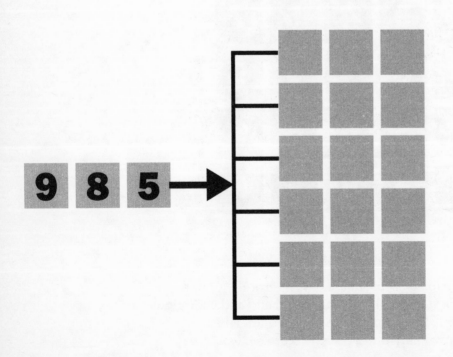

NUMBER PUZZLE 90

Place six three digit numbers of 100 plus at the end of 985 so that six numbers of six digits are produced. When each number is divided by 133 six whole numbers can be found. Which numbers should be placed in the grid?

ANSWER 12

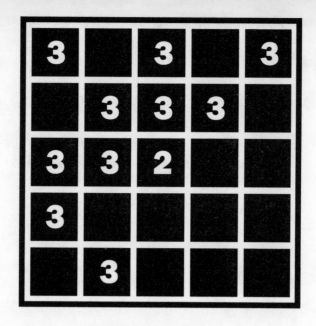

NUMBER PUZZLE 91

Each row, column and five-figure diagonal line
in this diagram must total 10. Three different numbers must be
used, as many times as necessary, to achieve this.
What are the numbers?

ANSWER 53

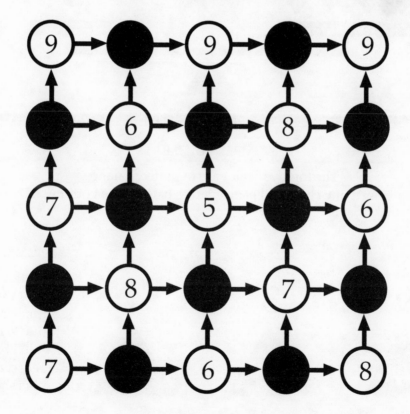

NUMBER PUZZLE 92

Move from the bottom left-hand corner to the top right-hand
corner following the arrows. Add the numbers on your route
together. If each black spot is worth minus 4,
what is the lowest number you can score?

ANSWER 1

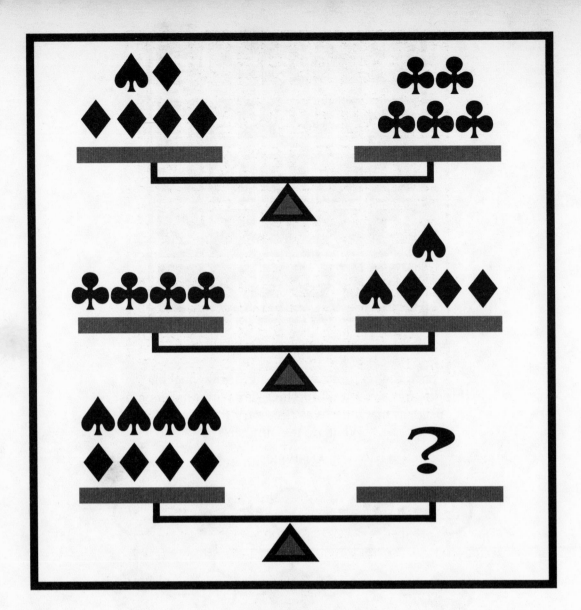

NUMBER PUZZLE 93

The top two scales are in perfect balance.
How many clubs will be needed to balance the bottom set?

ANSWER 42

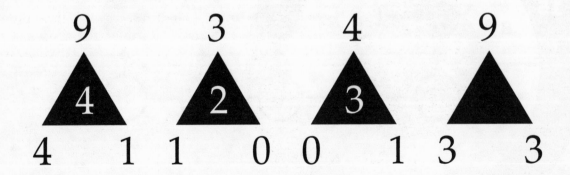

NUMBER PUZZLE 94

Which figure should be placed in the empty triangle?

ANSWER 94

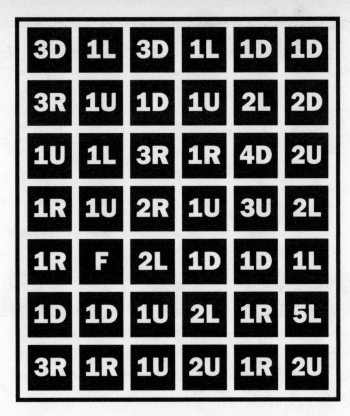

NUMBER PUZZLE 95

Here is an unusual safe. Each of the buttons must be pressed once
only in the correct order to open it. The last button is always
marked F. The number of moves and the direction is marked on
each button. Thus 1U would mean one move upwards
whilst 1L would mean one move to the left.
Which button is the first you must press?

ANSWER 83

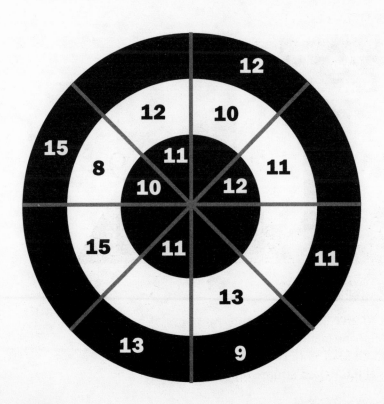

NUMBER PUZZLE 96

Complete the grid in such a way
that each segment of three numbers
totals the same.
When this has been done correctly
each of the three concentric circles of
eight numbers will produce three
identical totals.
Now complete the diagram.

ANSWER 31

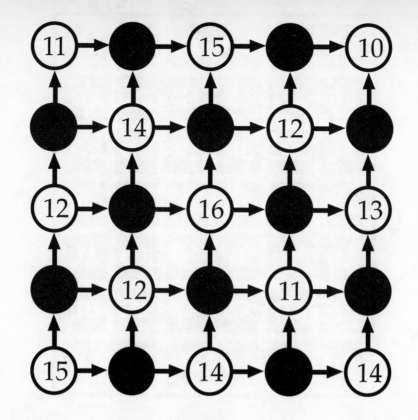

NUMBER PUZZLE 97

Move from the bottom left-hand corner to the top right-hand
corner following the arrows. Add the numbers on your route
together. If each black spot is worth minus 3,
which number can be scored only once?

ANSWER 73

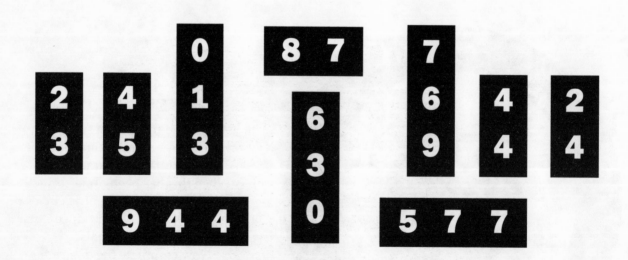

NUMBER PUZZLE 98

Place the tiles in a square to give some five-figure numbers. When
this has been done accurately the same
five numbers can be read both down and across.
How does the finished square look?

ANSWER 21

NUMBER PUZZLE 99

Start in the middle circle and move from circle to touching circle. Collect the four numbers which will total 30. Once a route has been found return to the middle circle and start again.
If a route can be found, which obeys the above rules but follows both a clockwise and an anticlockwise path, it is treated as two different routes. How many different ways are there?

ANSWER 63

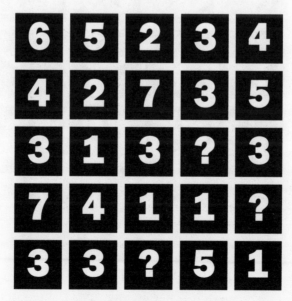

NUMBER PUZZLE 100

Which number should replace the question marks in the diagram?

ANSWER 11

NUMBER PUZZLE 101

You have four shots with each go to score 62. Aim at this target and work out how many different ways there are to make the score. Assume each shot scores and once four numbers have been used the same four cannot be used again in another order.
How many are there?

ANSWER 52

156

179

113

158

135 ? ? ?

NUMBER PUZZLE 102

The contents of each box has a value. The total of the values is shown alongside a row or beneath a column. Which number should replace the question mark?

ANSWER 104

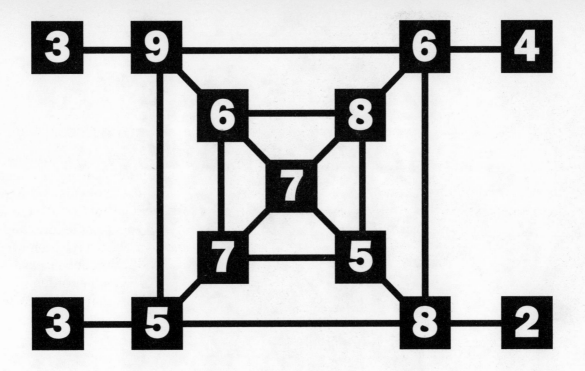

NUMBER PUZZLE 103

Start at the corner number and collect another four numbers by
following the paths shown. Add the five numbers together.
What is the lowest number you can score and how many times can
you score it?

ANSWER 93

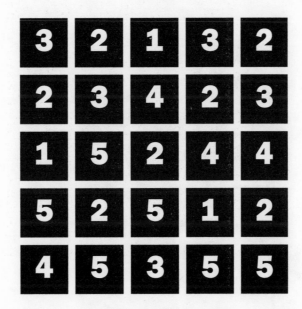

NUMBER PUZZLE 104

Move from square to adjacent square either vertically or
horizontally. Begin at the bottom left-hand square and end at the
top right-hand square. Collect nine numbers and total them.
How many different ways are there to total 31?

ANSWER 41

A B C D E

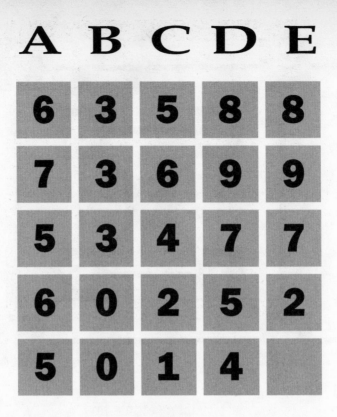

A	B	C	D	E
6	3	5	8	8
7	3	6	9	9
5	3	4	7	7
6	0	2	5	2
5	0	1	4	

NUMBER PUZZLE 103

There is a relationship between the columns of numbers in this diagram. The letters above the grid are there to help you. Which number should be placed in the empty squares?

ANSWER 102

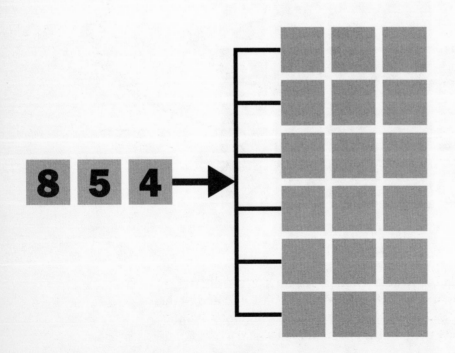

NUMBER PUZZLE 104

Six numbers must be placed in the blank space on the grid. Each number will be of three figures. The number given will then be attached to the front of each number so that a six-figure number will be produced. These new numbers, when divided by 149, will give six whole numbers. Which numbers must be placed in the grid?

ANSWER 51

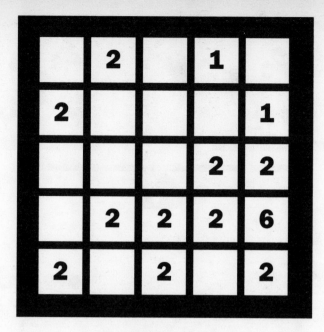

NUMBER PUZZLE 107

Each row, column and five-figure diagonal line
in this diagram must total 15. Three different numbers must be
used, as many times as necessary, to achieve this.
What are the numbers?

ANSWER 187

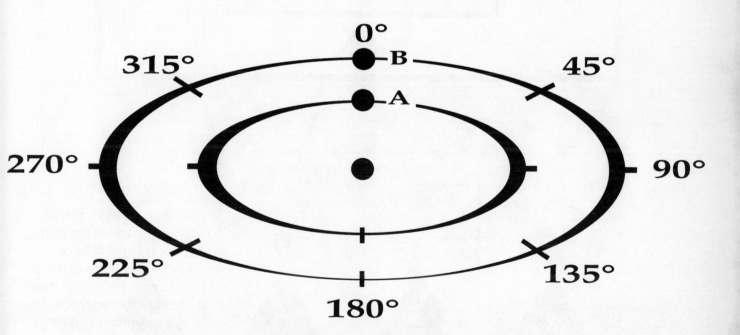

NUMBER PUZZLE 108

Two planets are in line with each other and the sun.
The outer planet will orbit the sun every one hundred years. The
inner planet takes twenty years. Both move in a clockwise
direction. When will they next form a straight line with each other
and the sun? The diagram should help you.

ANSWER 156

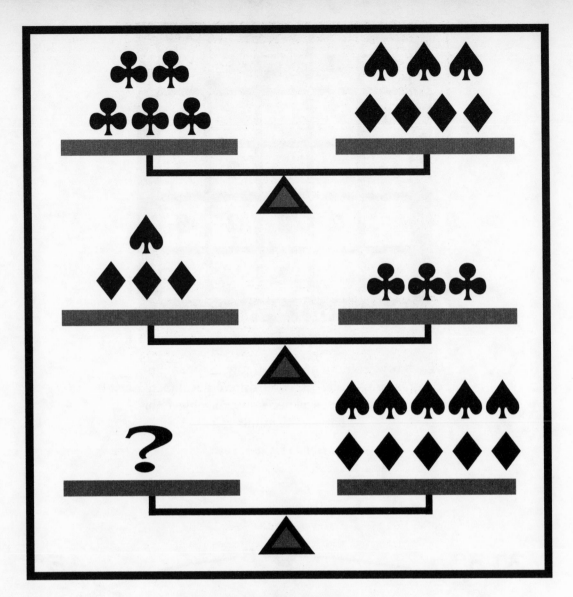

NUMBER PUZZLE 109

The top two scales are in perfect balance.
How many clubs will be needed to balance the bottom set?

ANSWER 197

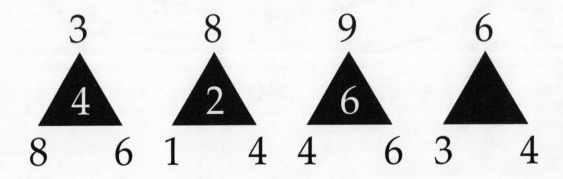

NUMBER PUZZLE 110

Which number should be placed in the empty triangle?

ANSWER 145

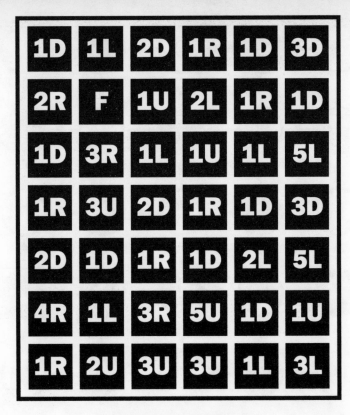

1D	1L	2D	1R	1D	3D
2R	F	1U	2L	1R	1D
1D	3R	1L	1U	1L	5L
1R	3U	2D	1R	1D	3D
2D	1D	1R	1D	2L	5L
4R	1L	3R	5U	1D	1U
1R	2U	3U	3U	1L	3L

NUMBER PUZZLE 111

Here is an unusual safe. Each of the buttons must be pressed once
only in the correct order to open it. The last button is always
marked F. The number of moves and the direction is marked on
each button. Thus 1U would mean one move up
whilst 1L would mean one move to the left.
Which button is the first you must press?

ANSWER 166

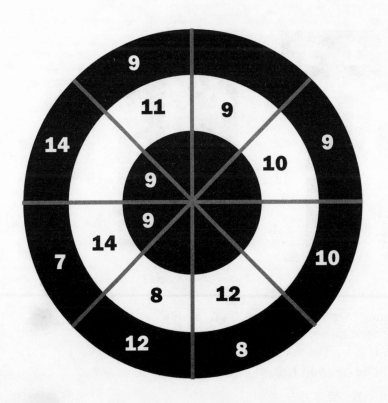

NUMBER PUZZLE 112

Complete the grid in such a way
that each segment of three numbers
totals the same.
When this has been done correctly
each of the three concentric circles of
eight numbers will produce
identical totals.
Now complete the diagram.

ANSWER 114

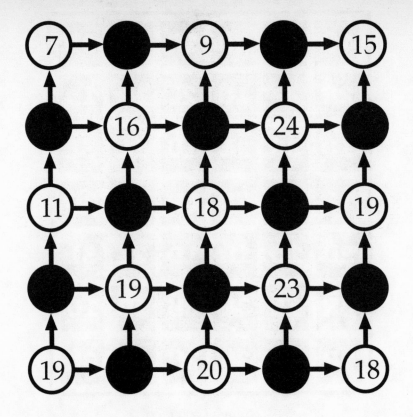

NUMBER PUZZLE 113

Move from the bottom left-hand corner to the top right-hand
corner following the arrows. Add the numbers on your route
together. If each black spot is worth minus 17,
how many different routes are there to score 2?

ANSWER 135

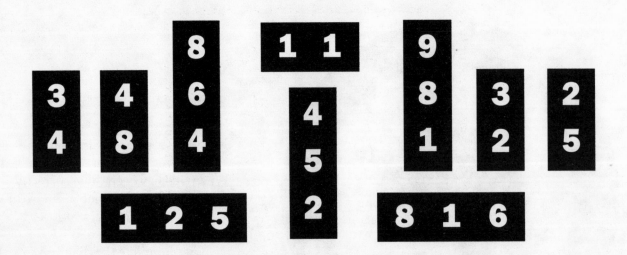

NUMBER PUZZLE 114

Place the tiles in a square to give some five-figure numbers.
When this has been done accurately the same
five numbers can be read both down and across.
How does the finished square look?

ANSWER 155

NUMBER PUZZLE 115

Start in the middle circle and move from circle to touching circle.
Collect the four numbers which will total 10. Once a route has
been found return to the middle circle and start again.
If a route can be found, which obeys the above rules but follows
both a clockwise and an anticlockwise path, it is treated as two
different routes. How many different ways are there?

ANSWER 196

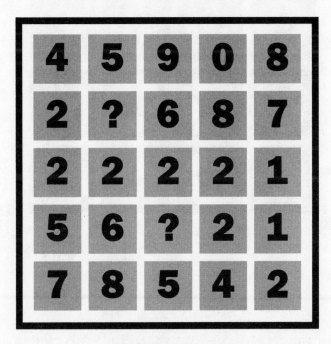

NUMBER PUZZLE 116

Which number should replace the question marks in the diagram?

ANSWER 144

NUMBER PUZZLE 117

You have five shots with each go to score 22. Aim at this target and work out how many different ways there are to make the score. Assume each shot scores and once five numbers have been used the same five cannot be used again in another order.
How many are there?

ANSWER 186

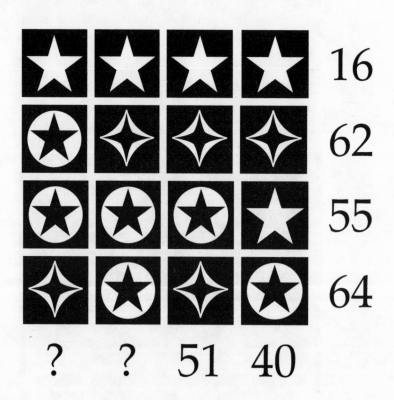

NUMBER PUZZLE 118

The contents of each box has a value. The total of the values is shown alongside a row or beneath a column. Which number should replace the question marks?

ANSWER 134

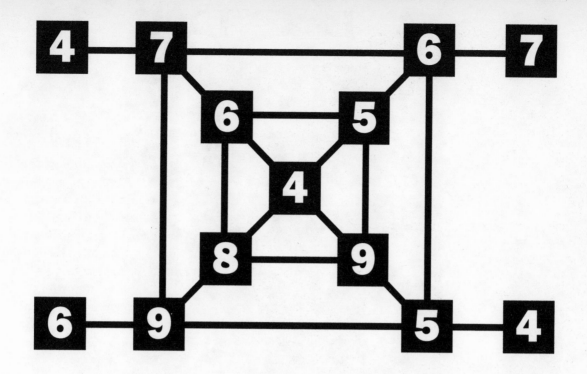

NUMBER PUZZLE 119

Start at any corner number and collect another four numbers by
following the paths shown. Add the five numbers together.
How many times can you score 37?

ANSWER 176

NUMBER PUZZLE 120

Move from square to adjacent square either vertically or
horizontally. Begin at the bottom left-hand square and end at the
top right-hand square. Collect nine numbers and total them.
How many different ways are there to total 46?

ANSWER 124

A B C D E

A	B	C	D	E
7	5	2	3	7
9	4	5	6	9
8	7	1	2	
8	4	4	5	
5	3	2	3	5

NUMBER PUZZLE 121

There is a relationship between the columns of numbers in this diagram. The letters above the grid are there to help you. Which number should be placed in the empty squares?

ANSWER 165

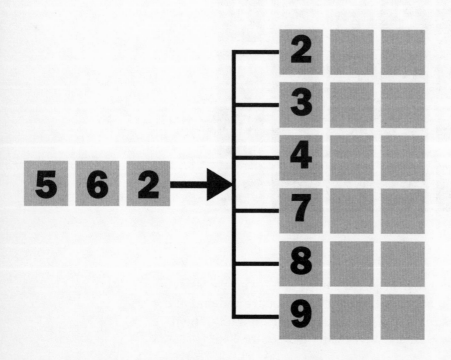

NUMBER PUZZLE 122

Place six three digit numbers of 100 plus at the end of 562 so that six numbers of six digits are produced. When each number is divided by 61.5 six whole numbers can be found. In this case, the first numbers are given. Which numbers should be placed in the grid?

ANSWER 113

NUMBER PUZZLE 123

Each row, column and five-figure diagonal line
in this diagram must total 20. Three different numbers must be
used, as many times as necessary, to achieve this.
What are the numbers?

ANSWER 125

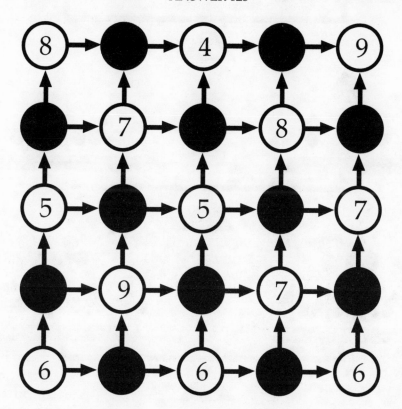

NUMBER PUZZLE 124

Move from the bottom left-hand corner to the top right-hand
corner following the arrows. Add the numbers on your route
together. If each black spot is worth minus 3,
how many different ways can you score 20?

ANSWER 154

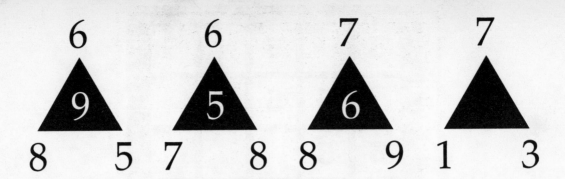

NUMBER PUZZLE 125

Which figure should be placed in the empty triangle?

ANSWER 143

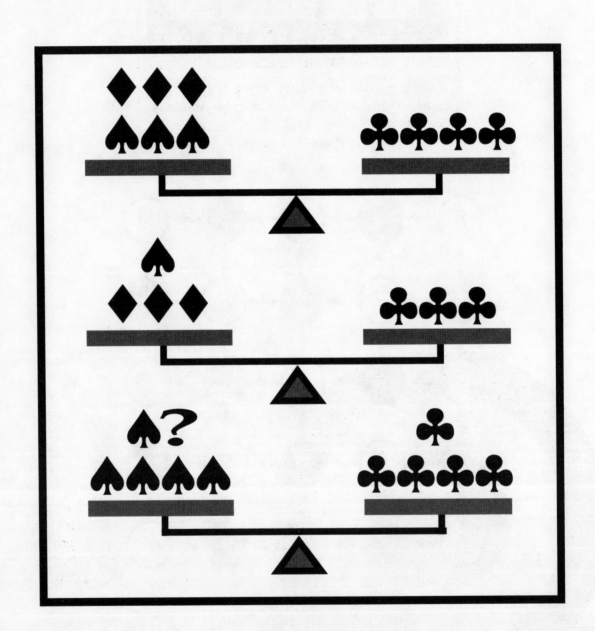

NUMBER PUZZLE 126

The top two scales are in perfect balance.
How many diamonds will be needed to balance the bottom set?

ANSWER 195

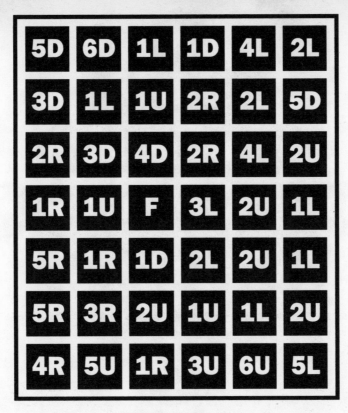

NUMBER PUZZLE 127

Here is an unusual safe. Each of the buttons must be pressed once
only in the correct order to open it. The last button is always
marked F. The number of moves and the direction is marked on
each button. Thus 1U would mean one move up
whilst 1L would mean one move to the left.
Which button is the first you must press?

ANSWER 185

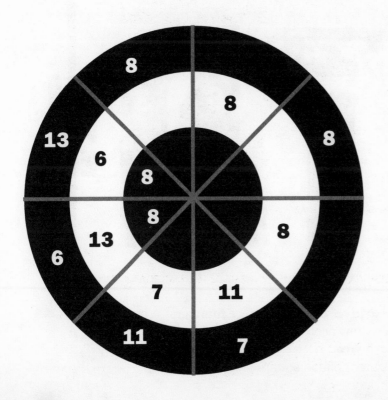

NUMBER PUZZLE 128

Complete the grid in such a way
that each segment of three numbers
totals the same.
When this has been done correctly
each of the three concentric circles of
eight numbers will produce
identical totals.
Now complete the diagram.

ANSWER 133

NUMBER PUZZLE 129

Start in the middle circle and move from circle to touching circle.
Collect the four numbers which will total 53. Once a route has
been found return to the middle circle and start again.
If a route can be found, which obeys the above rules but follows
both a clockwise and an anticlockwise path, it is treated as two
different routes. How many different ways are there?

ANSWER 175

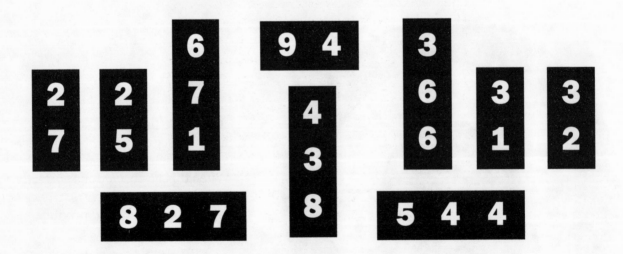

NUMBER PUZZLE 130

Place the tiles in a square to give some five-figure numbers. When
this has been done accurately the same
five numbers can be read both down and across.
How does the finished square look?

ANSWER 123

NUMBER PUZZLE 131

Start in the middle circle and move from circle to touching circle.
Collect the four numbers which will total 49. Once a route has
been found return to the middle circle and start again.
If a route can be found, which obeys the above rules but follows
both a clockwise and an anticlockwise path, it is treated as two
different routes. How many different ways are there?

ANSWER 164

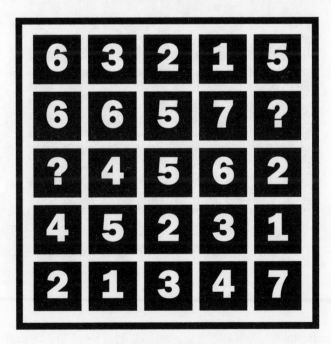

NUMBER PUZZLE 132

Which number should replace the question marks in the diagram?

ANSWER 112

NUMBER PUZZLE 133

You have five shots with each go to score 61. Aim at this target and work out how many different ways there are to make the score. Assume each shot scores and once five numbers have been used the same five cannot be used again in another order.
How many ways are there?

ANSWER 177

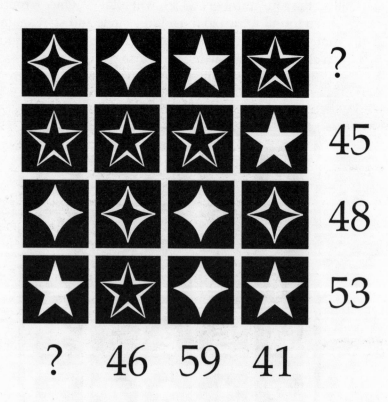

NUMBER PUZZLE 134

The contents of each box has a value. The total of the values is shown alongside a row or beneath a column. Which number should replace the question marks?

ANSWER 153

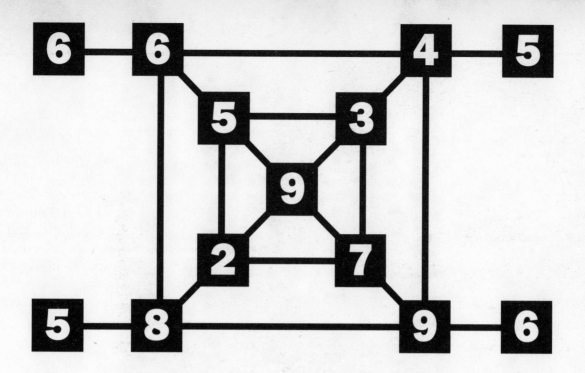

NUMBER PUZZLE 135

Start at any corner number and collect another four numbers by
following the paths shown. Add the five numbers together.
How many times can you score 38?

ANSWER 194

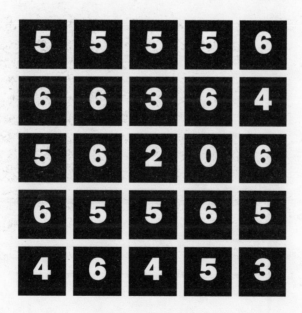

NUMBER PUZZLE 136

Move from square to adjacent square either vertically or
horizontally. Begin at the bottom left-hand square and end at the
top right-hand square. Collect nine numbers and total them.
How many different ways are there to total 48?

ANSWER 142

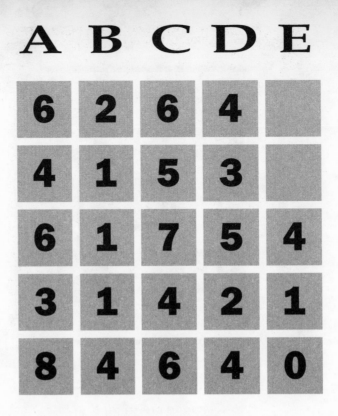

A B C D E

NUMBER PUZZLE 137

There is a relationship between the columns of numbers in this
diagram. The letters above the grid are there to help you.
Which number should be placed in the empty squares?

ANSWER 184

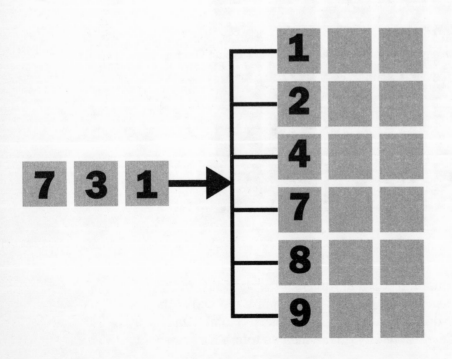

NUMBER PUZZLE 138

Place six three digit numbers of
100 plus at the end of 731 so that
six numbers of six digits are
produced. When each number is
divided by 39.5 six whole
numbers can be found. In this
case, the first numbers are given.
Which numbers should be
placed inthe grid?

ANSWER 132

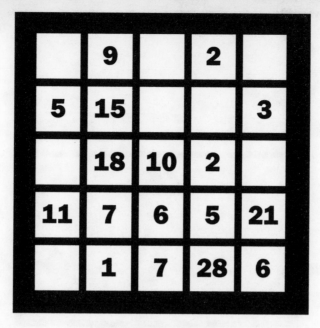

NUMBER PUZZLE 139

Each row, column and five-figure diagonal line
in this diagram must total 50. Four different numbers must be
used, as many times as necessary, to achieve this.
What are the numbers?

ANSWER 174

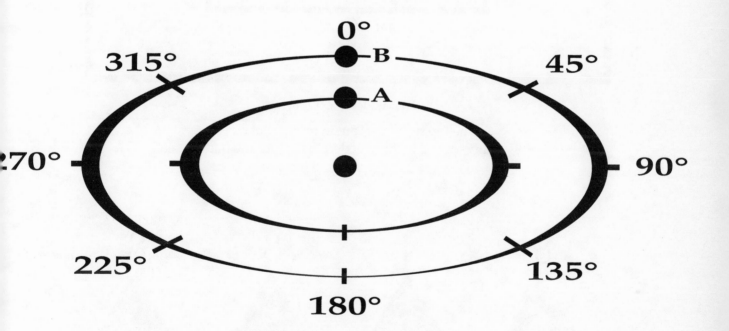

NUMBER PUZZLE 140

Two planets are in line with each other and the sun.
The outer planet will orbit the sun every 36 years. The inner
planet takes 4 years. Both move in a clockwise direction. When
will they next form a straight line with each other and the sun?
The diagram should help you.

ANSWER 122

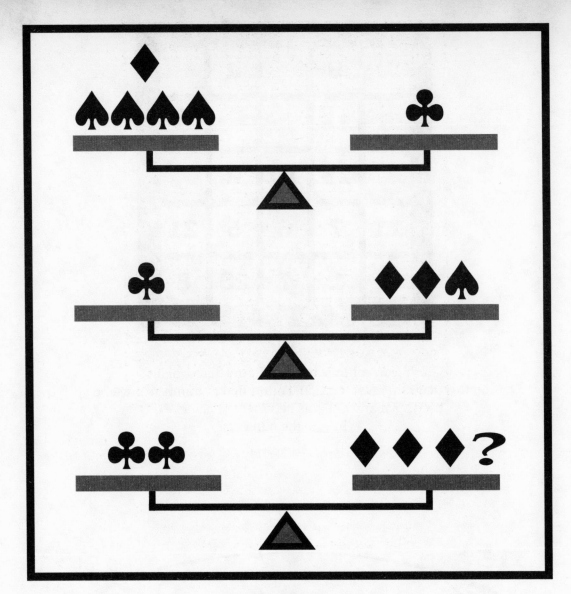

NUMBER PUZZLE 141

The top two scales are in perfect balance.
How many spades will be needed to balance the bottom set?

ANSWER 163

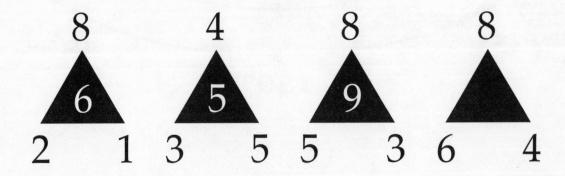

NUMBER PUZZLE 142

Which figure should be placed in the empty triangle?

ANSWER 111

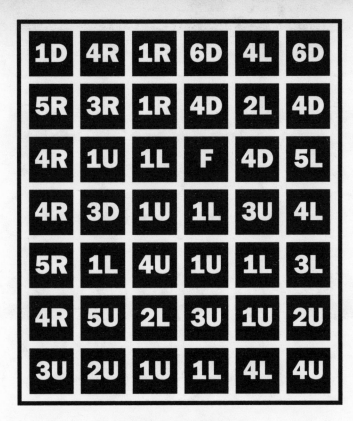

1D	4R	1R	6D	4L	6D
5R	3R	1R	4D	2L	4D
4R	1U	1L	F	4D	5L
4R	3D	1U	1L	3U	4L
5R	1L	4U	1U	1L	3L
4R	5U	2L	3U	1U	2U
3U	2U	1U	1L	4L	4U

NUMBER PUZZLE 143

Here is an unusual safe. Each of the buttons must be pressed once
only in the correct order to open it. The last button is always
marked F. The number of moves and the direction is marked on
each button. Thus 1U would mean one move up
whilst 1L would mean one move to the left.
Which button is the first you must press?

ANSWER 146

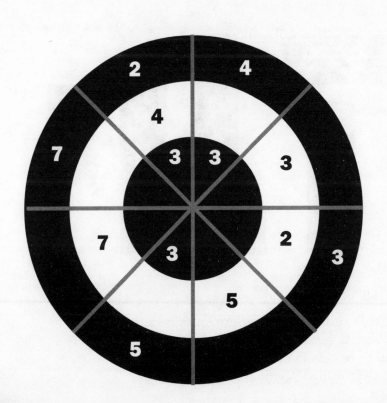

NUMBER PUZZLE 144

Complete the grid in such a way
that each segment of three numbers
totals the same.
When this has been done correctly
each of the three concentric circles of
eight numbers will produce
identical totals.
Now complete the diagram.

ANSWER 152

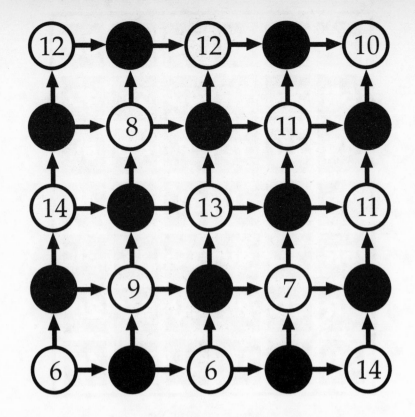

NUMBER PUZZLE 145

Move from the bottom left-hand corner to the top right-hand
corner following the arrows. Add the numbers on your route
together. If each black spot is worth minus 7,
how many different times can you score 22?

ANSWER 193

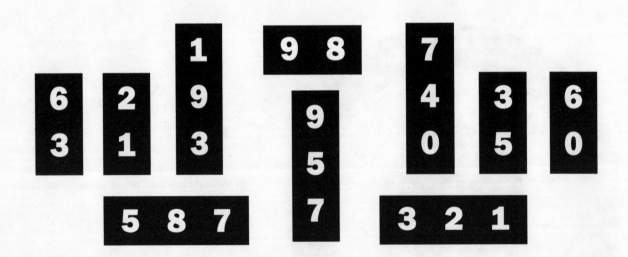

NUMBER PUZZLE 146

Place the tiles in a square to give some five-figure numbers.
When this has been done accurately the same
five numbers can be read both down and across.
How does the finished square look?

ANSWER 141

NUMBER PUZZLE 147

Start in the middle circle and move from circle to touching circle.
Collect the four numbers which will total 45. Once a route has
been found return to the middle circle and start again.
If a route can be found, which obeys the above rules but follows
both a clockwise and an anticlockwise path, it is treated as two
different routes. How many different ways are there?

ANSWER 183

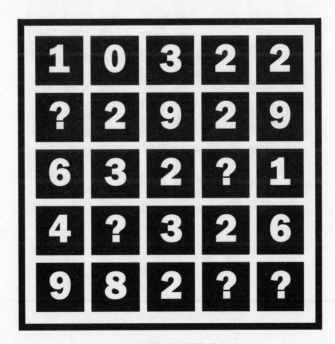

NUMBER PUZZLE 148

Which number should replace the question marks in the diagram?

ANSWER 131

NUMBER PUZZLE 149

You have three shots with each go to score 18. Aim at this target and work out how many different ways there are to make the score. Assume each shot scores and once three numbers have been used the same three cannot be used again in another order.
How many are there?

ANSWER 173

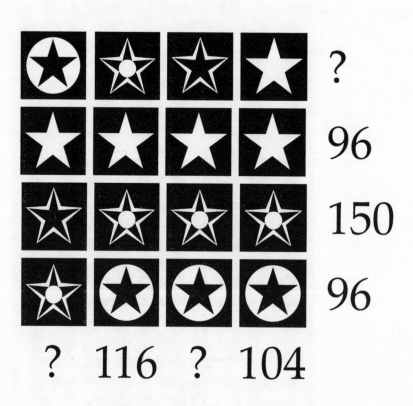

NUMBER PUZZLE 150

The contents of each box has a value. The total of the values is shown alongside a row or beneath a column. Which number should replace the question marks?

ANSWER 121

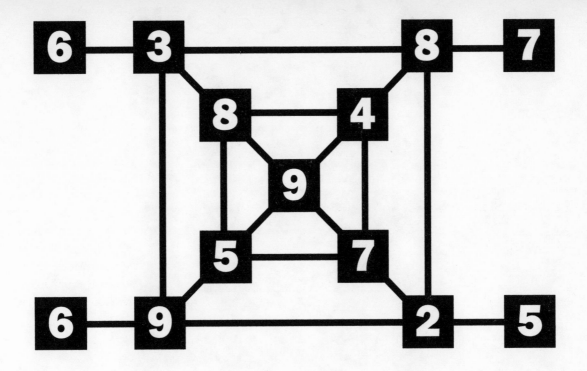

NUMBER PUZZLE 151

Start at any corner number and collect another four numbers by
following the paths shown. Add the five numbers together.
How many ways can you score 36?

ANSWER 162

NUMBER PUZZLE 152

Move from square to adjacent square either vertically or
horizontally. Begin at the bottom left-hand square and end at the
top right-hand square. Collect nine numbers and total them.
What is the highest score possible?

ANSWER 110

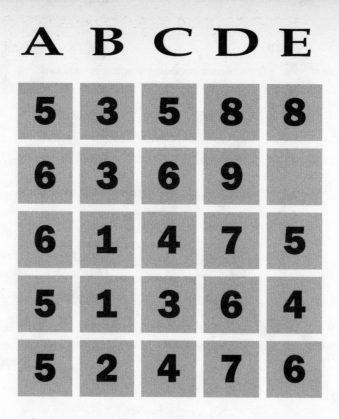

A	B	C	D	E
5	3	5	8	8
6	3	6	9	
6	1	4	7	5
5	1	3	6	4
5	2	4	7	6

NUMBER PUZZLE 153

There is a relationship between the columns of numbers in this diagram. The letters above the grid are there to help you. Which number should be placed in the empty square?

ANSWER 198

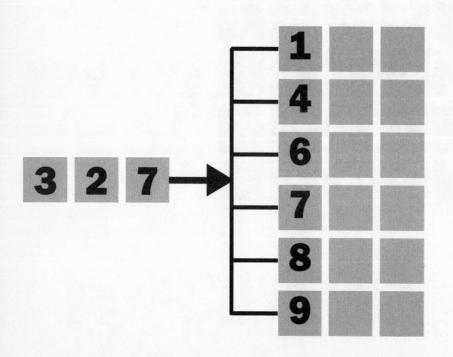

NUMBER PUZZLE 154

Place six three digit numbers of 100 plus at the end of 327 so that six numbers of six digits are produced. When each number is divided by 27.5 six whole numbers can be found. In this case, the first numbers are given. Which numbers should be placed inthe grid?

ANSWER 151

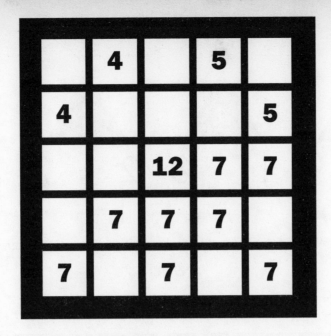

NUMBER PUZZLE 155

Each row, column and five-figure diagonal line
in this diagram must total 60. Three different numbers must
be used, as many times as necessary, to achieve this.
What are the numbers?

ANSWER 192

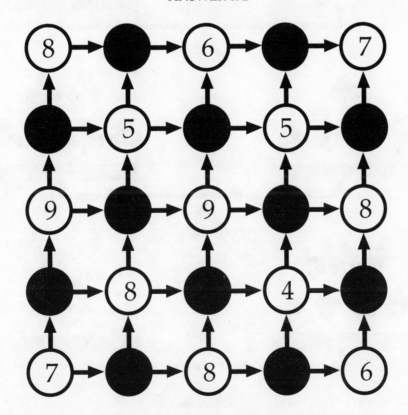

NUMBER PUZZLE 156

Move from the bottom left-hand corner to the top right-hand
corner following the arrows. Add the numbers on your route
together. If each black spot is worth 13,
which two numbers can be scored once only?

ANSWER 140

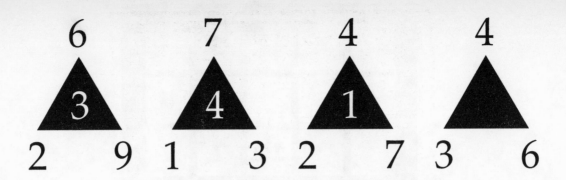

NUMBER PUZZLE 157

Which figure should be placed in the empty triangle?

ANSWER 130

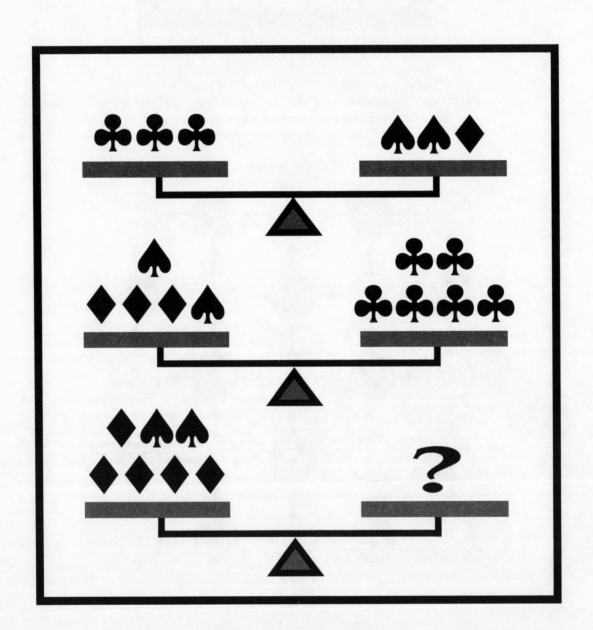

NUMBER PUZZLE 158

The top two scales are in perfect balance.
How many clubs will be needed to balance the bottom set?

ANSWER 182

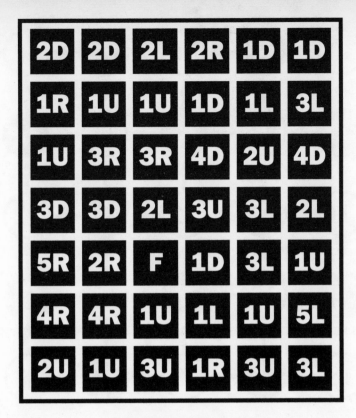

2D	2D	2L	2R	1D	1D
1R	1U	1U	1D	1L	3L
1U	3R	3R	4D	2U	4D
3D	3D	2L	3U	3L	2L
5R	2R	F	1D	3L	1U
4R	4R	1U	1L	1U	5L
2U	1U	3U	1R	3U	3L

NUMBER PUZZLE 159

Here is an unusual safe. Each of the buttons must be pressed once
only in the correct order to open it. The last button is always
marked F. The number of moves and the direction is marked on
each button. Thus 1U would mean one move up
whilst 1L would mean one move to the left.
Which button is the first you must press?

ANSWER 172

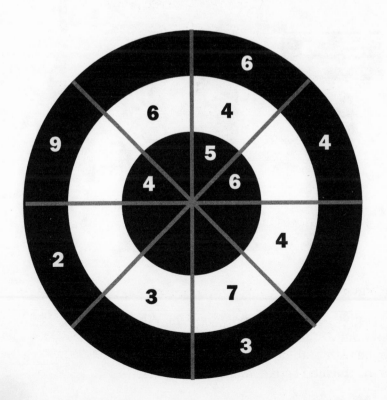

NUMBER PUZZLE 160

Complete the grid in such a way
that each segment of three numbers
totals the same.
When this has been done correctly
each of the three concentric circles of
eight numbers will produce
identical totals.
Now complete the diagram.

ANSWER 120

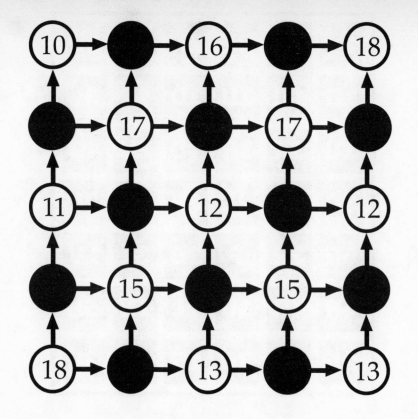

NUMBER PUZZLE 161

Move from the bottom left-hand corner to the top right-hand
corner following the arrows. Add the numbers on your route
together. If each black spot is worth minus 9,
how many times can you score 41?

ANSWER 161

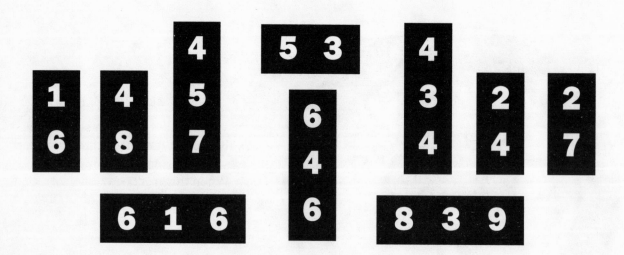

NUMBER PUZZLE 162

Place the tiles in a square to give some five-figure numbers. When
this has been done accurately the same
five numbers can be read both down and across.
How does the finished square look?

ANSWER 109

NUMBER PUZZLE 163

Start in the middle circle and move from circle to touching circle.
Collect the four numbers which will total 75. Once a route has
been found return to the middle circle and start again.
If a route can be found, which obeys the above rules but follows
both a clockwise and an anticlockwise path, it is treated as two
different routes. How many different ways are there?

ANSWER 202

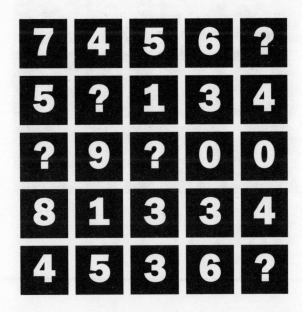

NUMBER PUZZLE 164

Which number should replace the question marks in the diagram?

ANSWER 150

NUMBER PUZZLE 165

You have five shots with each go to score 56. Aim at this target and work out how many different ways there are to make the score. Assume each shot scores and once five numbers have been used the same five cannot be used again in another order.
How many ways are there?

ANSWER 191

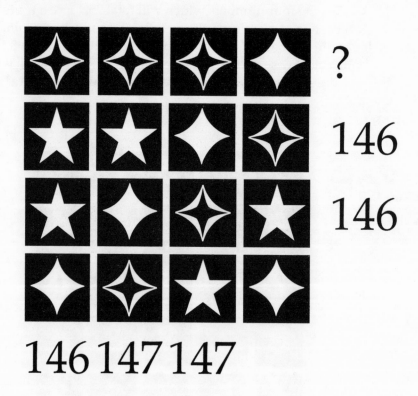

NUMBER PUZZLE 166

The contents of each box has a value. The total of the values is shown alongside a row or beneath a column. Which number should replace the question mark?

ANSWER 139

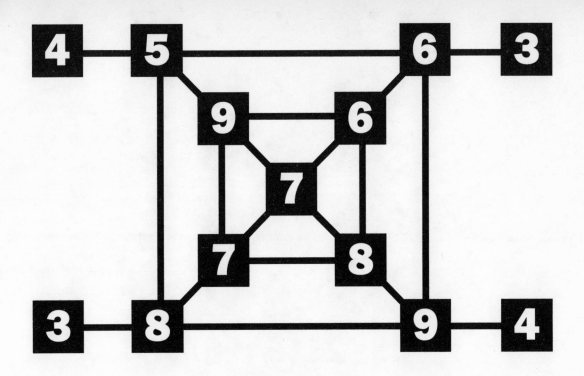

NUMBER PUZZLE 167

Start at any corner number and collect another four numbers by
following the paths shown. Add the five numbers together.
How many times can you score less than 30?

ANSWER 181

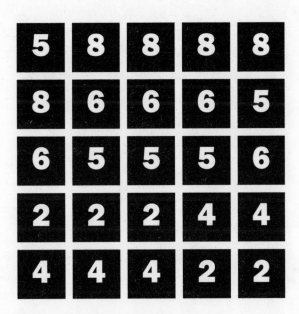

NUMBER PUZZLE 168

Move from square to adjacent square either vertically or horizontally. Begin at the bottom left-hand square and end at the top
right-hand square. Collect nine numbers and total them.
What are the highest and lowest numbers you can score?

ANSWER 129

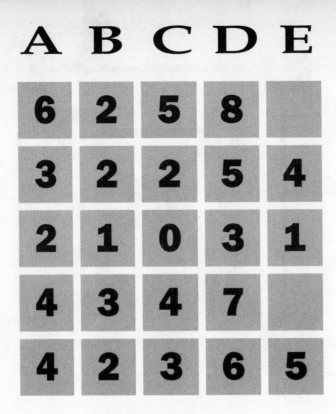

A B C D E

NUMBER PUZZLE 169

There is a relationship between the columns of numbers in this diagram. The letters above the grid are there to help you. Which number should be placed in the empty squares?

ANSWER 171

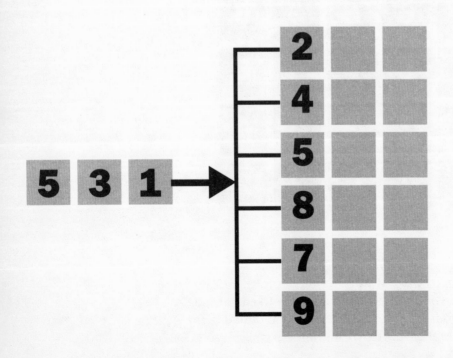

NUMBER PUZZLE 170

Place six three digit numbers of 100 plus at the end of 531 so that six numbers of six digits are produced. When each number is divided by 40.5 six whole numbers can be found. In this case, the first numbers are given. Which numbers should be placed in the grid?

ANSWER 119

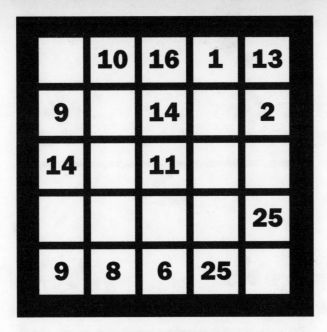

NUMBER PUZZLE 171

Each row, column and five-figure diagonal line
in this diagram must total 55. Three different numbers must be
used, as many times as necessary, to achieve this.
What are these numbers?

ANSWER 160

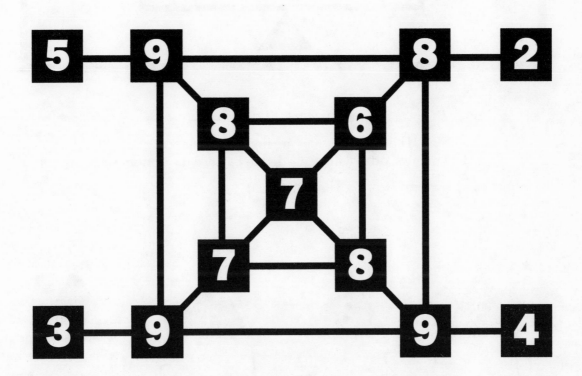

NUMBER PUZZLE 172

Start at any corner number and collect another four numbers by
following the paths shown. Add the five numbers together.
How many times can you score 40?

ANSWER 108

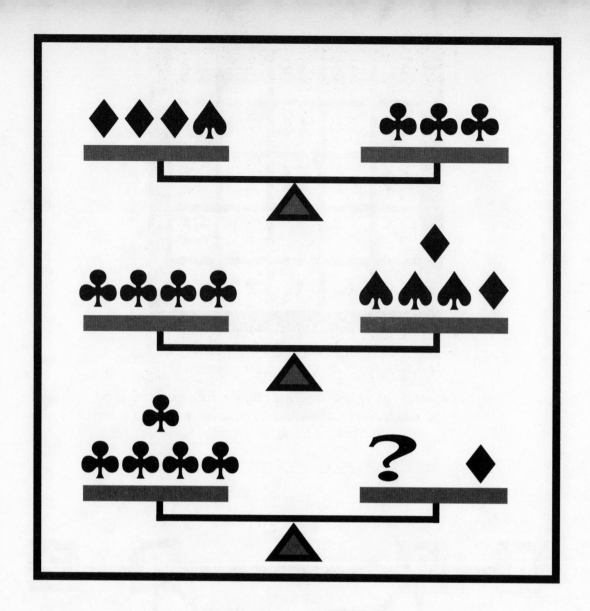

NUMBER PUZZLE 173

The top two scales are in perfect balance.
How many spades will be needed to balance the bottom set?

ANSWER 201

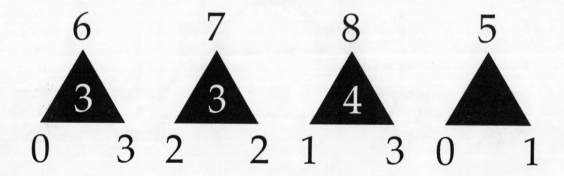

NUMBER PUZZLE 174

Which figure should be placed in the empty triangle?

ANSWER 149

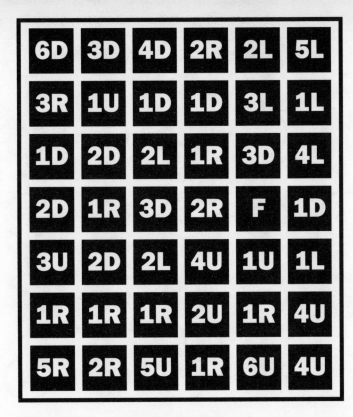

6D	3D	4D	2R	2L	5L
3R	1U	1D	1D	3L	1L
1D	2D	2L	1R	3D	4L
2D	1R	3D	2R	F	1D
3U	2D	2L	4U	1U	1L
1R	1R	1R	2U	1R	4U
5R	2R	5U	1R	6U	4U

NUMBER PUZZLE 175

Here is an unusual safe. Each of the buttons must be pressed once
only in the correct order to open it. The last button is always
marked F. The number of moves and the direction is marked on
each button. Thus 1U would mean one move up
whilst 1L would mean one move to the left.
Which button is the first you must press?

ANSWER 190

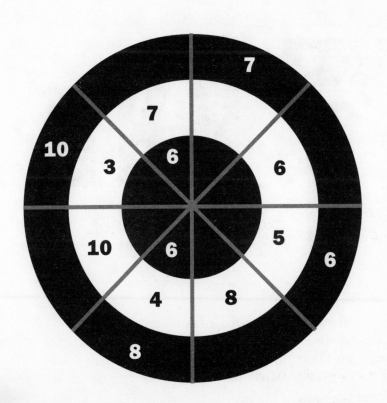

NUMBER PUZZLE 176

Complete the grid in such a way
that each segment of three numbers
totals the same.
When this has been done correctly
each of the three concentric circles of
eight numbers will produce
identical totals.
Now complete the diagram.

ANSWER 138

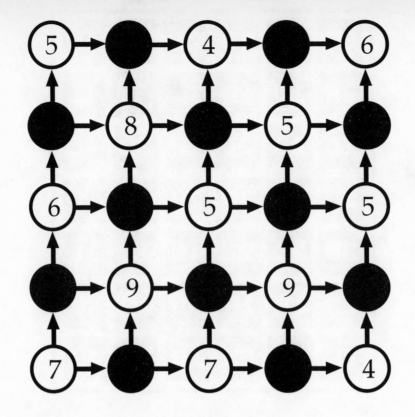

NUMBER PUZZLE 177

Move from the bottom left-hand corner to the top right-hand
corner following the arrows. Add the numbers on your route
together. If each black spot is worth 11,
how many times can you score 80?

ANSWER 180

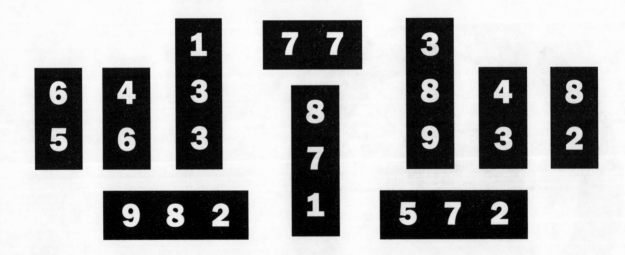

NUMBER PUZZLE 178

Place the tiles in the square to give some five-figure numbers.
When this has been done accurately the same
five numbers can be read both down and across.
How does the finished square look?

ANSWER 128

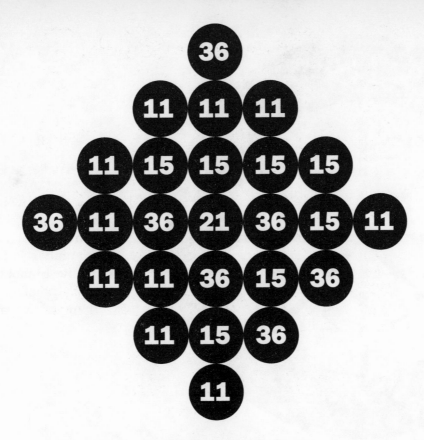

NUMBER PUZZLE 179

Start in the middle circle and move from circle to touching circle.
Collect the four numbers which will total 83. Once a route has
been found return to the middle circle and start again.
If a route can be found, which obeys the above rules but follows
both a clockwise and an anticlockwise path, it is treated as two
different routes.
How many different ways are there?

ANSWER 170

NUMBER PUZZLE 180

Which number should replace the question mark in the diagram?

ANSWER 118

NUMBER PUZZLE 181

You have five shots with each go to score 44. Aim at this target and work out how many different ways there are to make the score. Assume each shot scores and once five numbers have been used the same five cannot be used again in another order.
How many ways are there?

ANSWER 159

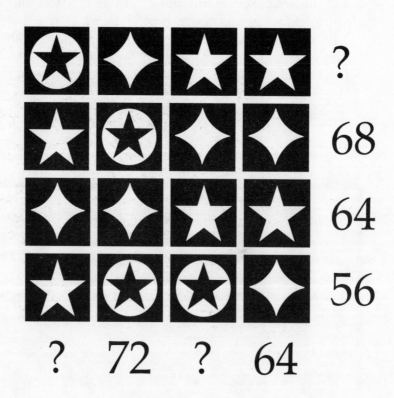

NUMBER PUZZLE 182

The contents of each box has a value. The total of the values is shown alongside a row or beneath a column. Which number should replace the question marks?

ANSWER 107

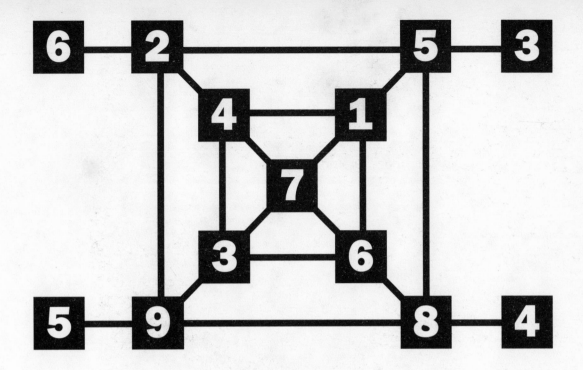

NUMBER PUZZLE 183

Start at any corner number and collect another four numbers by
following the paths shown. Add the five numbers together.
What is the lowest number you can score?

ANSWER 200

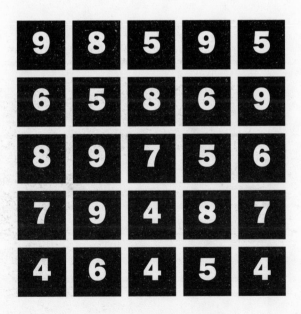

NUMBER PUZZLE 184

Move from square to adjacent square either vertically or horizontally. Begin at the bottom left-hand square and end at the top right-
hand square. Collect nine numbers and total them.
Which total can be scored only once?

ANSWER 148

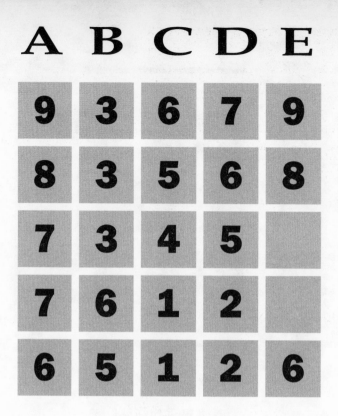

A B C D E

9	3	6	7	9
8	3	5	6	8
7	3	4	5	
7	6	1	2	
6	5	1	2	6

NUMBER PUZZLE 185

There is a relationship between the columns of numbers in this
diagram. The letters above the grid are there to help you.
Which number should be placed in the empty squares?

ANSWER 189

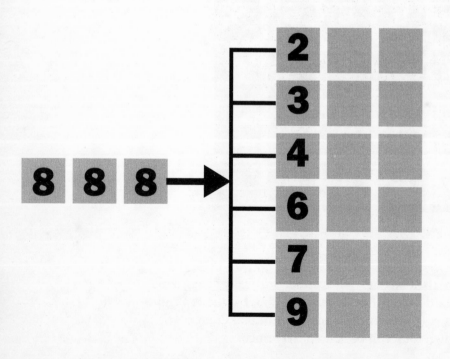

NUMBER PUZZLE 186

Place six three digit numbers of
100 plus at the end of 888 so that
six numbers of six digits are
produced. When each number is
divided by 77 six whole
numbers can be found. In this
case, the first numbers are given.
Which numbers should be
placed inthe grid?

ANSWER 137

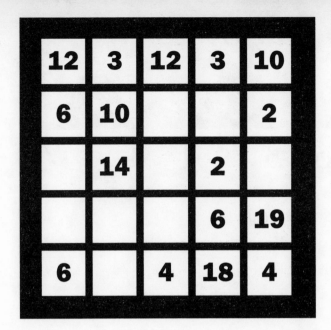

NUMBER PUZZLE 187

Each row, column and five-figure
diagonal line in this diagram must
total 40. Three different numbers
must be used, as many times as necessary, to achieve this.
What are the numbers?

ANSWER 179

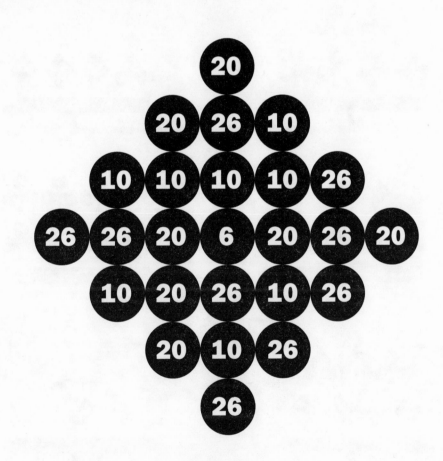

NUMBER PUZZLE 188

Start in the middle circle and move from circle to touching circle.
Collect the four numbers which will total 62. Once a route has been
found return to the middle circle and start again.
If a route can be found, which obeys the above rules
but follows both a clockwise and an anticlockwise path,
it is treated as two different routes.
How many different ways are there?

ANSWER 127

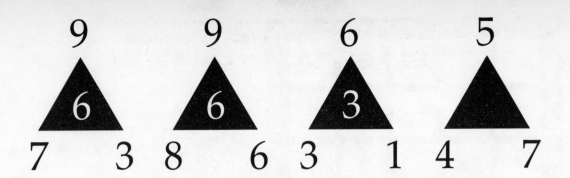

NUMBER PUZZLE 189

Which figure should be placed in the empty triangle?

ANSWER 117

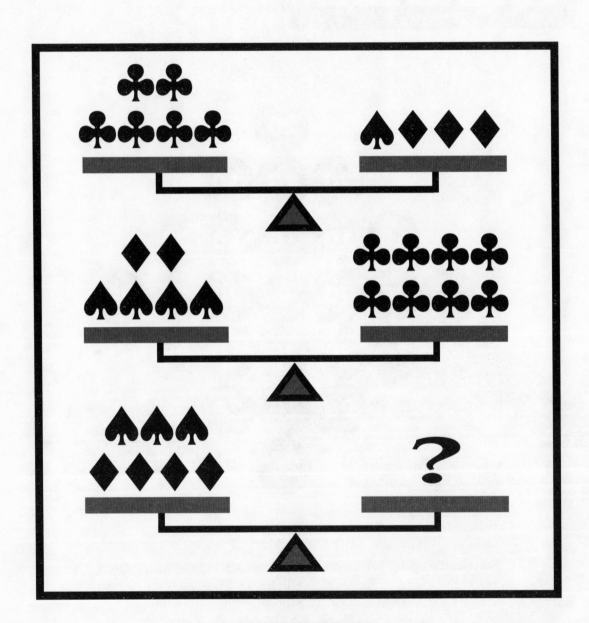

NUMBER PUZZLE 190

The top two scales are in perfect balance.
How many clubs will be needed to balance the bottom set?

ANSWER 169

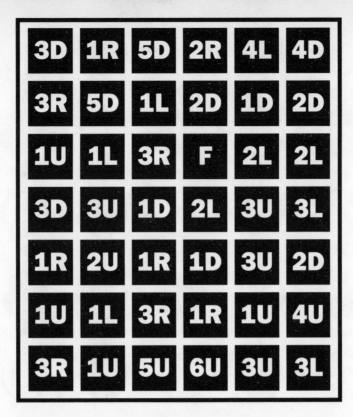

3D	1R	5D	2R	4L	4D
3R	5D	1L	2D	1D	2D
1U	1L	3R	F	2L	2L
3D	3U	1D	2L	3U	3L
1R	2U	1R	1D	3U	2D
1U	1L	3R	1R	1U	4U
3R	1U	5U	6U	3U	3L

NUMBER PUZZLE 191

Here is an unusual safe. Each of the buttons must be pressed once
only in the correct order to open it. The last button is always
marked F. The number of moves and the direction is marked on
each button. Thus 1U would mean one move up
whilst 1L would mean one move to the left.
Which button is the first you must press?

ANSWER 158

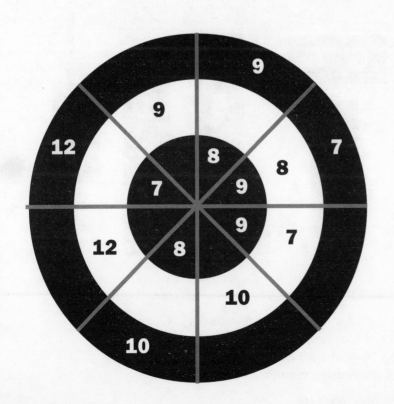

NUMBER PUZZLE 192

Complete the grid in such a way
that each segment of three numbers
totals the same.
When this has been done correctly
each of the three concentric circles of
eight numbers will produce
identical totals.
Now complete the diagram.

ANSWER 106

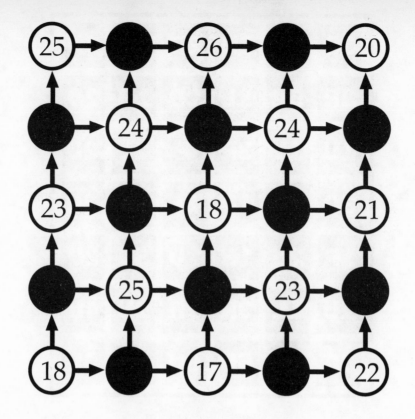

NUMBER PUZZLE 193

Move from the bottom left-hand corner to the top right-hand corner following the arrows. Add the numbers on your route together. If each black spot is worth minus 19, how many times can you score 24?

ANSWER 199

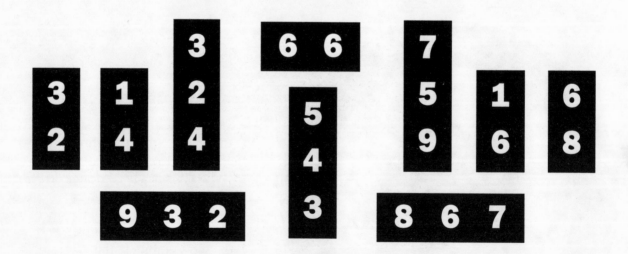

NUMBER PUZZLE 194

Place the tiles a square to give some five-figure numbers. When this has been done accurately the same five numbers can be read both down and across. How does the finished square look?

ANSWER 147

NUMBER PUZZLE 195

Start in the middle circle and move from circle to touching circle.
Collect the four numbers which will total 90. Once a route has
been found return to the middle circle and start again.
If a route can be found, which obeys the above rules but follows
both a clockwise and an anticlockwise path, it is treated as two
different routes. How many different ways are there?

ANSWER 188

NUMBER PUZZLE 196

Which number should replace the question marks in the diagram?

ANSWER 136

NUMBER PUZZLE 197

You have three shots with each go to score 36. Aim at this target and work out how many different ways there are to make the score. Assume each shot scores and once three numbers have been used the same three cannot be used again in another order.
How many are there?

ANSWER 178

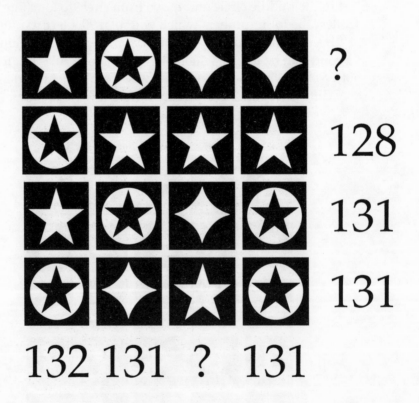

NUMBER PUZZLE 198

The contents of each box has a value. The total of the values is shown alongside a row or beneath a column. Which numbers should replace the question marks?

ANSWER 126

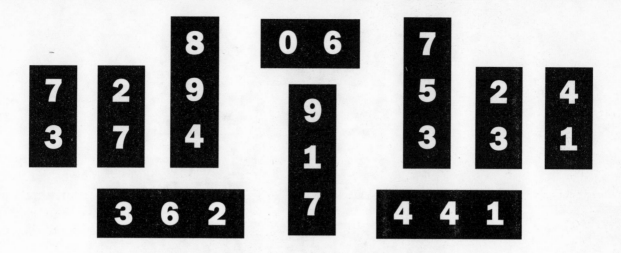

NUMBER PUZZLE 199

Place the tiles in a square to give some five-figure numbers.
When this has been done accurately the same
five numbers can be read both down and across.
How does the finished square look?

ANSWER 168

NUMBER PUZZLE 200

Move from square to adjacent square either vertically or
horizontally. Begin at the bottom left-hand square and end at the
top right-hand square. Collect nine numbers and total them.
How many different ways are there to total 39?

ANSWER 116

A B C D E

	A	B	C	D	E
	9	0	6	9	
	8	1	6	9	7
	7	2	6	9	8
	7	1	5	8	
	3	1	1	4	2

NUMBER PUZZLE 201

There is a relationship between the columns of numbers in this diagram. The letters above the grid are there to help you. Which number should be placed in the empty squares?

ANSWER 157

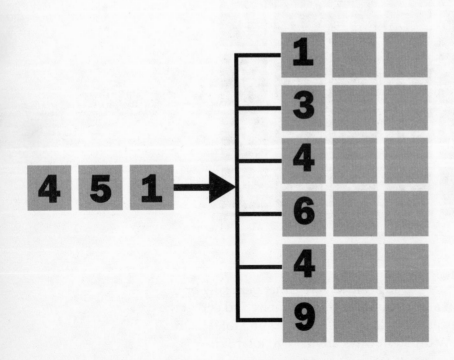

NUMBER PUZZLE 202

Place six three digit numbers of 100 plus at the end of 451 so that six numbers of six digits are produced. When each number is divided by 61 six whole numbers can be found. In this case, the first numbers are given. Which numbers should be placed inthe grid?

ANSWER 105

Answers

1   17.

2

3   29.

4   10. The top number is multiplied by the bottom left-hand number and the total is divided by the bottom right-hand number.

5   1. The top row minus the bottom row gives the third row. The bottom row plus the second row gives the fourth row.

6   164
    295
    426
    557
    688
    819

7   Our answer is:

8   11 ways.

9   In two years time. The outer planet is 60 degrees in its orbit, the sun is in the middle and the inner planet is at 240 degrees.

10

11   8. The top row minus the bottom row gives the third row. The third row plus the second row gives the fourth row.

12   131
    264
    397
    663
    796
    929

13   Our answer is:

14   107 (values of symbols: ✦ = 18, ✦ = 30, ☆ = 29).

15   Once.

16

17   Once.

18   7. The top number is multiplied by the bottom left number and the bottom right number is taken away from this total to give the middle number.

19   5. 3rd row - top row = 5th row. 4th row + 5th row = 2nd.row.

20   162
    313
    464
    615
    766
    917

21

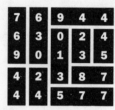

22   Three times.

23   4. The top number is added to the bottom left-hand number and the bottom right-hand number is subtracted.

24   6. The top row plus the second row gives the third row. The second row plus the fourth row gives the fifth row.

25   314
    425
    536
    647
    758
    869

26   Our answer is:

27   149 (values of symbols: ✦ = 35, ✦ = 42, ☆ = 37).

28   3 times.

29

30   3 ways.

31   Our answer is:

32   65 (values of symbols: ☢ = 7, ◈ = 8, ★ = 25, ☆ = 17).

33   In three and three-quarter years' time. The outer planet is 90 degrees in its orbit, the sun is in the middle and the inner planet is at 270 degrees.

34

35   Once.

36   3. The top number minus the bottom left-hand number is multiplied by the bottom right-hand number.

37   1. The second row plus the third row gives the top row. The third row plus the fourth row gives the bottom row.

38   431
        542
        653
        764
        875
        986

39   Our answer is:

40   62 (values of symbols: ◈ = 13, ★ = 21, ✦ = 7).

41   6 ways.

42   7 clubs.

43   8. The middle row minus the bottom row equals the top row.

44   232
        354
        476
        598
        842
        964

45   Our answer is:

46   78 (values of symbols: ☢ = 28, ☆ = 13, ▦ = 9).

47   In one and a half years' time. The outer planet is 90 degrees in its orbit, the sun is in the middle and the inner planet is at 270 degrees.

48

49   2 ways.

50   6. The bottom two numbers are added and taken from the top number.

51   5. Take the bottom row from the middle row to give the top row.

52   27 ways.

53   0, 1 and 4.

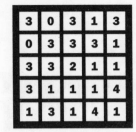

54   Four.

55   40.

56   4 spades.

57   10 ways.

58   2. A + B = D. A - B = C. D - C = E.

59   4U on the third row from the bottom.

60   204 (values of symbols: ☆ = 44, ☢ = 58, ◈ = 45).

61   10, 11, 23 and 31.

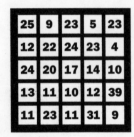

62   5 times.

63   14 ways.

64   4. A + B = D. A - B = C. D - C = E.

65   1L in the second column from the left one row from the bottom.

66   8 ways.

67   9, 17 and 18.

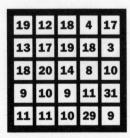

68   Four routes.

69   30.

70   7 clubs.

71   12 ways.

72   2. A + B = D. A - B = C. D - C = E.

73   58.

74   40 and once.

75   6 clubs.

76   7 ways.

77   4. A - B + 1 = D. D - 1 = C. D + B - 1 = E.

78   1L in the third column from the left on the third row from the bottom.

79   15 ways.

80   11, 12 and 21.

19	12	22	6	21
9	21	23	20	7
20	21	16	11	12
21	12	9	11	27
11	14	10	32	13

81   4 times.

82   37.

83   1U in the second column from the left on the second row.

84   7 ways.

85   9 and 17.

17	10	17	4	17
8	17	19	17	4
17	22	13	4	9
14	9	7	9	26
9	7	9	31	9

86   2 routes.

87   4 times.

88   4 diamonds.

89   7 ways.

90   3. A - B = D. C = D + 2. E = D - B.

91   1D fourth from the left on the top row.

92   11 ways.

93   27 and twice.

94   3. The top number minus the bottom left-hand number minus the bottom right-hand number.

95   7 ways.

96   5. A - B = D. D + 2 = C. D - B = E.

97   3U on the bottom row.

98   21 ways.

99   11, 18 and 19.

19	13	21	3	19
14	19	20	18	4
20	23	15	7	10
11	12	10	11	31
11	8	9	36	11

100   One.

101   Twice.

102   5 clubs.

103   5 ways.

104   157 (values of symbols: ⊛ = 45, ◆ = 44, ☆ = 23).

105. 156
     339
     461
     644
     400
     949

106. Our answer is:

107. 52 (values of symbols: ⊛ = 12, ☆ = 8, ◆ = 24).

108. 3 times.

109.

6	4	6	1	6
4	3	4	2	4
6	4	5	7	8
1	2	7	5	3
6	4	8	3	9

110. 60.

111. 8. The top number minus the bottom left–hand number multiplied by the right–hand number.

112. 8. 3rd row - top row = 5th row. 5th row + 4th row = 2nd row.

113. 233
     356
     479
     725
     848
     971

114. Our answer is:

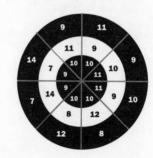

115. 217
     366
     515
     664
     813
     962

116. 2 times.

117. 7. The top number minus the bottom left–hand number multiplied by the right hand number.

118. 3. Top row + bottom row = middle row.

119. 279
     441
     522
     846
     765
     927

120. Our answer is:

121. 122 (values of symbols ⊛ = 20, ☆ = 24, ✦ = 42, ✰ = 36).

122. In 2 ¼ years time. The outer planet is 22.5 degrees in its orbit, the sun is in the middle and the inner planet is at 202.5 degrees.

123.

124. 2 ways.

125. 1, 3, and 4.

126. 126 at the side and 122 beneath (values of symbols: ☆ = 31, ◆ = 30, ✪ = 35).

127. 11 ways.

128.

129. 58 and 37.

130. 6. The top number multiplied by the bottom left–hand number minus the right–hand number.

131. 5. The top row plus the second row gives the third row. The second row plus the fourth gives the fifth row.

132. 145
224
461
777
856
935

133. Our answer is:

134. 53 (values of symbols: ☆ = 4, ✪ = 17, ✧ = 15).

135. 4 routes.

136. 6. 2nd row + 3rd row = top row. 3rd row + 4th row = 5th row.

137. 272
349
426
657
734
965

138. Our answer is:

139. 148 (values of symbols: ✧ = 38, ☆ = 37, ◆ = 34).

140. 90 and 92.

141.

142. 4 ways.

143. 5. The top number is added to the bottom left–hand number and the bottom right–hand number is subtracted.

144. 3. The top row is the total of the 2nd and 3rd rows. The bottom row is the total of the 3rd and 4th rows.

145. 4 ½. The top number multiplied by the bottom left–hand number divided by the bottom right–hand number.

146. 5U on the second row from the bottom.

147.

148. 54.

149. 4. The top number minus the two bottom numbers combined.

150. 2. The top row minus the bottom row gives the third row. The third row plus the second row gives the fourth row.

151. 195
415
635
745
855
965

152. Our answer is:

153. 47 (values of symbols ✧ = 6, ★ = 11, ☆ = 12, ◆ = 18).

154. 2 ways.

155.

156. In twelve and a half years time. The outer planet is 45 degrees in its orbit, the sun is in the middle and the inner planet is at 225 degrees.

157. 6. A + B = D. D – 3 = C. C + B = E.

158. 3U on the bottom row.

159. 34 ways.

160. 7, 8 and 15.

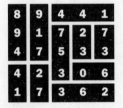

161. Once.

162. 2 ways.

163. 5 spades.

164. 9 ways.

165. 8. A − B + 1 = D. D − 1 = C. B + C = E.

166. 3D on the top row.

167. 1. A + B − 1 = D. D − 3 = C. B + C = E

168.

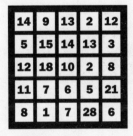

169. 10 clubs.

170. 7 ways.

171. 7. A + B = D. D − 3 = C. C + B = E.

172. 3R in the third column from the left on the third row down.

173. 7 ways.

174. 8, 12, 13 and 14.

175. 19 ways.

176. 4 times.

177. 37 ways.

178. 9 ways.

179. 5, 8 and 11.

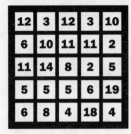

180. 8 times.

181. 6 times.

182. 9 clubs.

183. 7 ways.

184. 2. A − B = D. D + 2 = C. D − B = E

185. 2R on the third row down in the fourth column from the left.

186. 59 ways.

187. 3, 4 and 6.

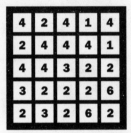

188. 13 ways.

189. 7. A − B = C. C + 1 = D. B + C = E.

190. 4U on the third row from the bottom.

191. 21 ways.

192. 15, 17 and 24.

193. 8 times.

194. Once.

195. 3 diamonds.

196. 7 ways.

197. 7 clubs.

198. 9. A + B = D. D − 3 = C. C + B = E..

199. Once.

200. 15.

201. 5 spades

202. 4 ways.

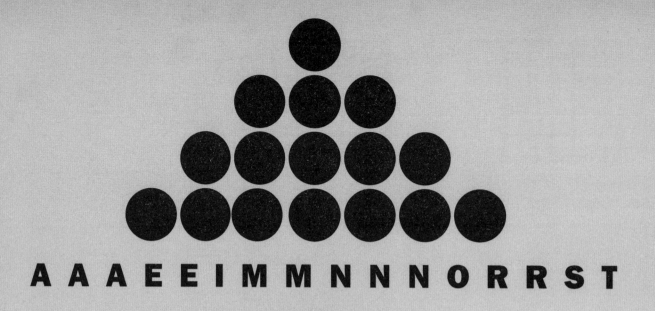

AAAEEIMMNNNORRST

16 LONDON   YORK 11

23 LIVERPOOL   BIRMINGHAM ?

O V
C
C K
A E

N E
E
W
K
N
C O
B A

INTRODUCTION TO WORD PUZZLES

Puzzles which involve the use of of the English language are notoriously difficult to produce. Unfortunately the differences between the English used in Europe and the English used elsewhere are considerable. This book uses words which, hopefully, match the use of English throughout the world. The main dictionaries used are *Webster's New World Dictionary* and the *Collins English Dictionary*.

Word puzzles are fun. This has been proved over and over again in the many puzzle features which have been printed in major newspapers and magazines throughout the world. At the time of writing the British Rail first-class magazine, Intercity, prints a page of similar puzzles each issue. A British national newspaper carries a puzzle per day, and this is in the process of worldwide syndication. Many in-flight magazines from the far-east to the Caribbean use similar puzzles. My problem is that I have to devise them. Fortunately I have an extremely able helper in Carolyn Skitt. She checks, criticizes and improves on many of the puzzles produced. Without Carolyn this book would still be in the making. Help has also come from other quarters. Joanne Harris spent a great deal of time perfecting the tinted puzzles, Bobby Raikhy worked on the many diagrammatic styles, and David Ballheimer checked the proofs. But what of Mensa?

If you can solve the puzzles can you join the organization? You should have no problem. These are fun puzzles but by no means easy. If you can work these out, the Mensa test should prove to be no hurdle and you should easily qualify. Once you have joined, you will find a feeling of satisfaction that very few experience in a lifetime. You will meet people of all walks of life but of similar brain power. A scientist can meet a poet; a composer, an architect. The broadening of intellectual vision is amazing. The new horizon is formidable, but challenging. I invite you to join this ever-expanding group of people, where race, religion or political pesuasion are not blocks but keys: keys to opening new doors of understanding, friendship and considered discussion.

There are 40,000 Mensa members in the British Isles alone. There are over 50,000 in the USA. There are 120,000 throughout the world. Write to Mensa, Mensa House, St John's Square, Wolverhampton WV2 1AH, England, or American Mensa Limited at 2626 E 14th Street, Brooklyn, New York 11235-3992, USA.

Harold Gale
Former Executive Director of British Mensa
March,1993

WORD PUZZLE 1

Place one letter in the middle of this diagram. Four five-letter
words can now be rearranged from each straight line of letters.
What is the letter and what are the words?

ANSWER 62

WORD PUZZLE 2

Arrange the tiles in this diagram so that they form a square.
When this is done correctly four words can be read down and
across. What are the words?

ANSWER 10

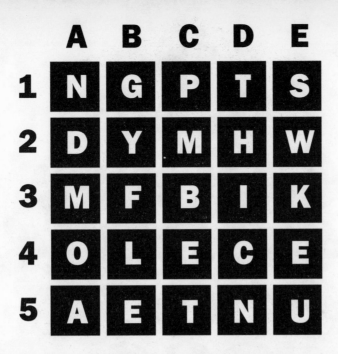

	A	B	C	D	E
1	N	G	P	T	S
2	D	Y	M	H	W
3	M	F	B	I	K
4	O	L	E	C	E
5	A	E	T	N	U

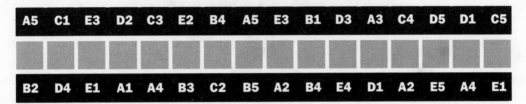

A5	C1	E3	D2	C3	E2	B4	A5	E3	B1	D3	A3	C4	D5	D1	C5
B2	D4	E1	A1	A4	B3	C2	B5	A2	B4	E4	D1	A2	E5	A4	E1

WORD PUZZLE 3

Select one of the two letters from the grid, in accordance with the reference shown, and place it in the word frame. When the correct letters have been chosen a sixteen-letter word can be read.
What is the word?

ANSWER 103

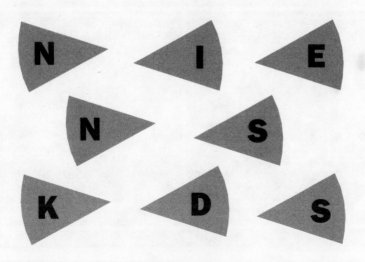

WORD PUZZLE 4

Make a circle out of these shapes.
When the correct circle has been found an English word can be read clockwise. What is the word?

ANSWER 51

WORD PUZZLE 5

Move from circle to touching circle collecting the letters of GOLD.
Always start at the G.
How many different ways are there to do this?

ANSWER 92

BEAST	ADDER
DECOR	PILAF
HERON	PYGMY
BATON	TAXIS
HUMAN	ROUND

WORD PUZZLE 6

Six of the words in the diagram are associated for some
reason. Find the words and then work out whether SHELL belongs
to the group.

ANSWER 40

WORD PUZZLE 7

Change the second letter of each word to the left and the right.
Two other English words must be formed. Place the letter used in
the empty section. When this has been completed for all the words
another English word can be read down. What is the word?

ANSWER 82

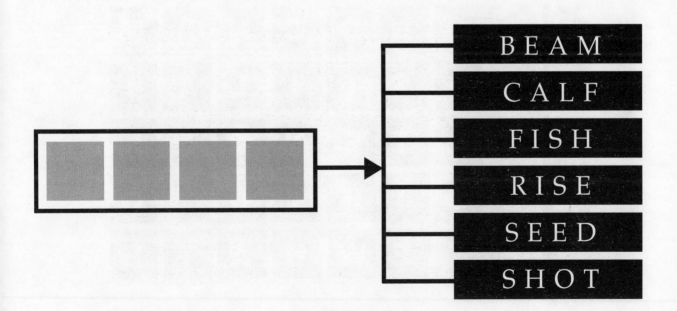

WORD PUZZLE 8

Which English word of four letters can be attached to the front of
the words shown in the diagram to create six other words?

ANSWER 30

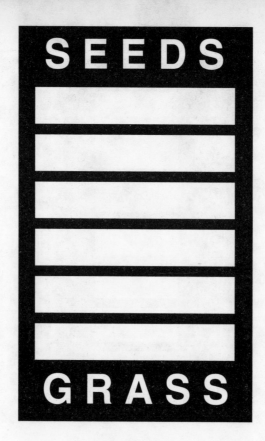

SEEDS

GRASS

WORD PUZZLE 9

Complete the word ladder by changing one letter of each word per step. The newly created word must be found in the dictionary. What are the words to turn SEEDS to GRASS?

ANSWER 72

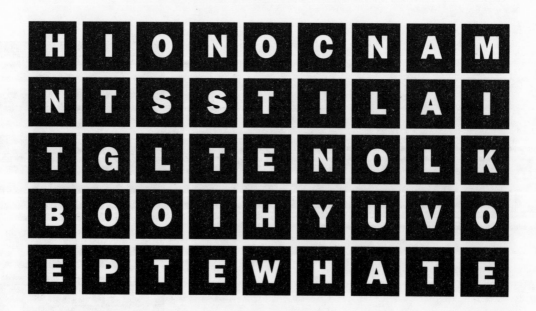

H	I	O	N	O	C	N	A	M
N	T	S	S	T	I	L	A	I
T	G	L	T	E	N	O	L	K
B	O	O	I	H	Y	U	V	O
E	P	T	E	W	H	A	T	E

WORD PUZZLE 10

A quotation has been written in this diagram. Find the start letter and move from square to touching square until you have found it. What is the quotation and to whom is it attributed?

ANSWER 20

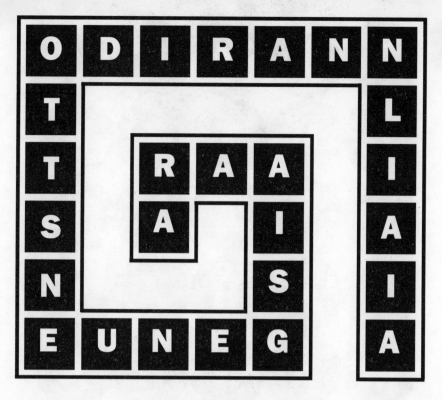

WORD PUZZLE 11

The names of three countries are to be found in the diagram.
The letters of the names are in the order they normally appear.
What are the countries?

ANSWER 61

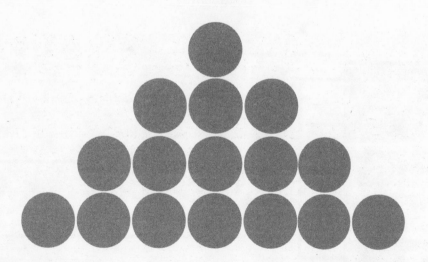

A A D D I I I L L L Q T U V W Y

WORD PUZZLE 12

Place the letters shown into the diagram in such a way
that three words can be read across and one down the middle.
What are the words?

ANSWER 9

WORD PUZZLE 13

Start at the bottom letter M and move from circle to touching circle
to the N at the top right. How many different ways are there of collecting the nine letters of MANHATTAN?

ANSWER 102

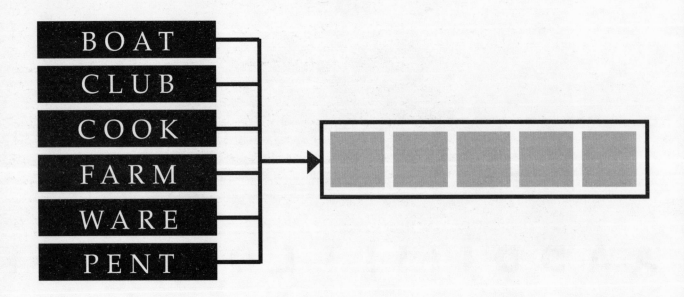

WORD PUZZLE 14

Which English word of five letters can be attached to the back of
the words shown in the diagram to create six other words?

ANSWER 50

WORD PUZZLE 15

Select one letter from each of the segments.
When the correct letters have been found a word of eight letters
can be read clockwise. What is the word?

ANSWER 91

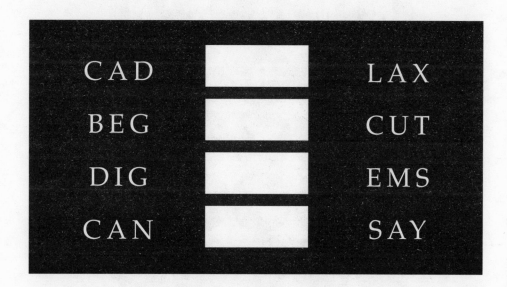

CAD		LAX
BEG		CUT
DIG		EMS
CAN		SAY

WORD PUZZLE 16

Place two letters in the empty space which, when added to the
end of the words to the left and to the beginning of the right, form
other English words. When this is completed another word
can be read downwards. What is the word?

ANSWER 39

N O F S
Q O E E
C A R Y
M U T S

WORD PUZZLE 17

Take the letters and arrange them correctly in the column under which they appear. Once this has been done an historical character will appear. Who is the person?

ANSWER 81

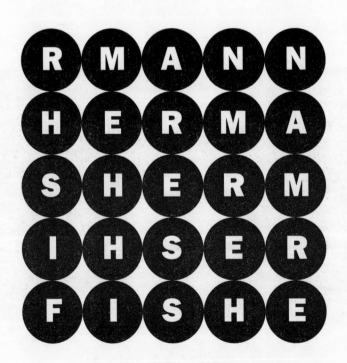

WORD PUZZLE 18

Start at the bottom letter F and move from circle to touching circle to the N at the top right. How many different ways are there of collecting the nine letters of FISHERMAN?

ANSWER 29

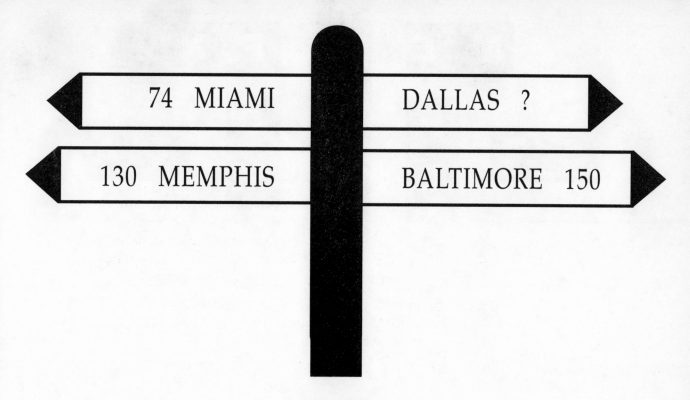

WORD PUZZLE 19

This is a meaningless signpost but there is a twisted form of
logic behind the figures. Discover the logic and find the distance to
Dallas. How far is it?

ANSWER 71

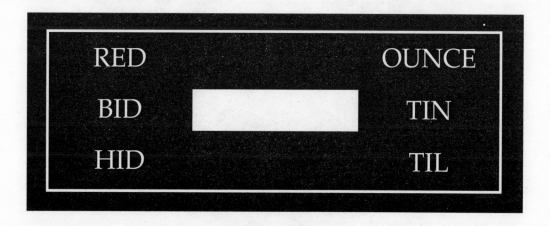

WORD PUZZLE 20

Place an English word of THREE letters in the empty space. This
word, when added to the end of the three words to the left and to
the beginning of the three words to the right, will form six other
words. What is the word?

ANSWER 19

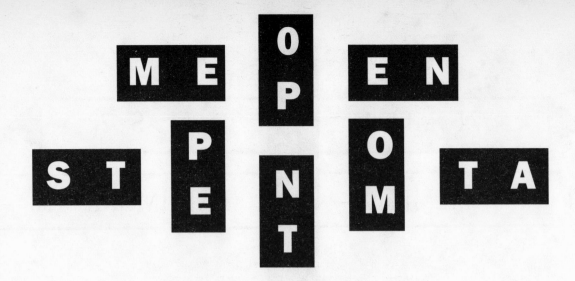

WORD PUZZLE 21

Arrange the tiles in this diagram so that they form a square.
When this is done correctly four words can be read down and
across. What are the words?

ANSWER 8

WORD PUZZLE 22

Place one letter in the middle of this diagram. Four five-letter
words can now be rearranged from each straight line of letters.
What is the letter and what are the words?

ANSWER 60

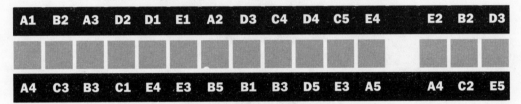

WORD PUZZLE 23

Select one of the two letters from the grid, in accordance with the reference shown, and place it in the word frame. When the correct letters have been chosen an occasion can be read. What is the occasion?

ANSWER 101

WORD PUZZLE 24

Make a circle out of these shapes.
When the correct circle has been found an English word can be read clockwise. What is the word?

ANSWER 49

BURNT	EVENT
COUNT	CADET
MERIT	FAULT
FLINT	CARAT
ABBOT	GIANT

WORD PUZZLE 25

Five of the words in the diagram are associated for some
reason. Find the words and then work out whether PLANT
belongs to the group.

ANSWER 90

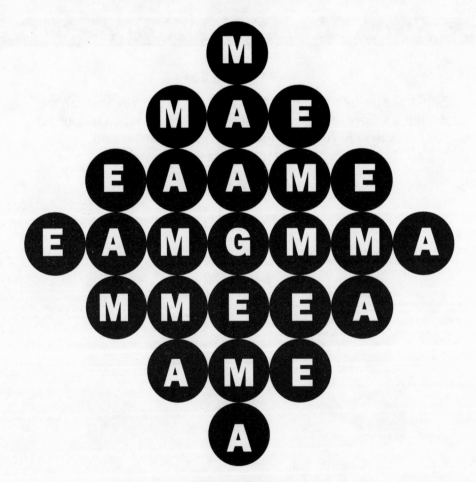

WORD PUZZLE 26

Move from circle to touching circle collecting the letters of GAME.
Always start at the G.
How many different ways are there to do this?

ANSWER 38

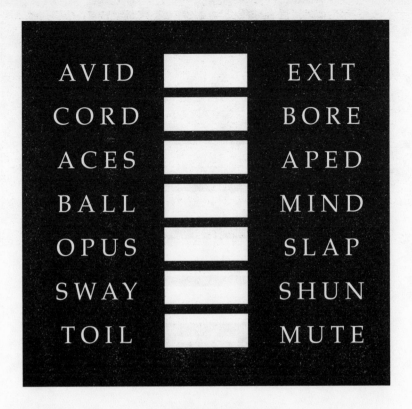

WORD PUZZLE 27

Change the second letter of each word to the left and the right.
Two other English words must be formed. Place the letter used in
the empty section. When this has been completed for all the words
another English word can be read down. What is the word?

ANSWER 80

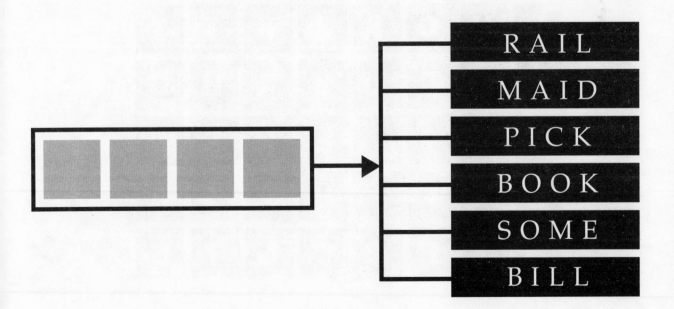

WORD PUZZLE 28

Which English word of four letters can be attached to the front of
the words shown in the diagram to create six other words?

ANSWER 28

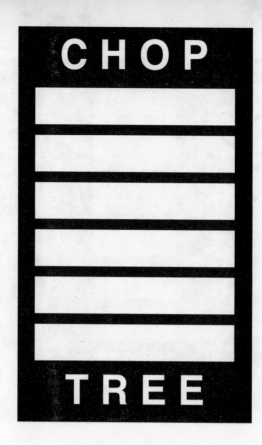

WORD PUZZLE 29

Complete the word ladder by changing one letter of each word
per step. The newly created word must be found in the dictionary.
What are the words to turn CHOP to TREE?

ANSWER 70

WORD PUZZLE 30

A quotation has been written in this diagram. Find the start letter
and move from square to touching square until you have found it.
What is the quotation and to whom is it attributed?

ANSWER 18

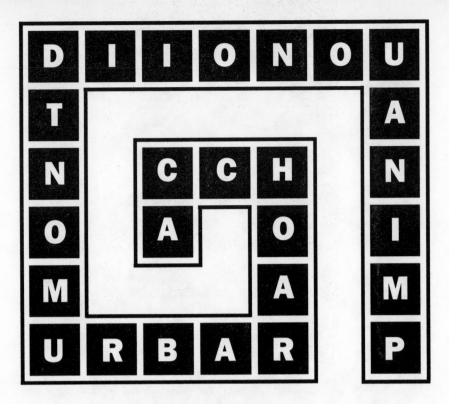

WORD PUZZLE 31

The names of four musical instruments are to be found in the diagram. The letters of the names are in the order they normally appear. What are the musical instruments?

ANSWER 59

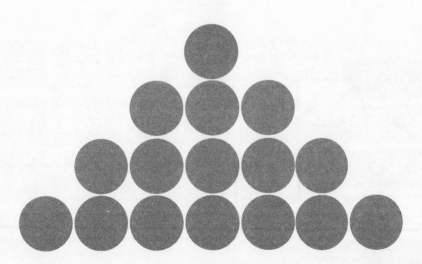

A E F F F F I I I M R R R R S T

WORD PUZZLE 32

Place the letters shown into the diagram in such a way that three words can be read across and one down the middle. What are the words?

ANSWER 7

WORD PUZZLE 33

Start at the bottom letter N and move from circle to touching circle
to the E at the top right. How many different ways are there of
collecting the nine letters of NECTARINE?

ANSWER 100

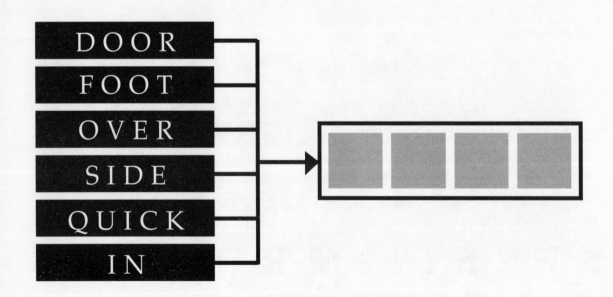

WORD PUZZLE 34

Which English word of four letters can be attached to the back of
the words shown in the diagram to create six other words?

ANSWER 48

WORD PUZZLE 35

Select one letter from each of the segments.
When the correct letters have been found a word of eight letters
can be read clockwise. What is the word?

ANSWER 89

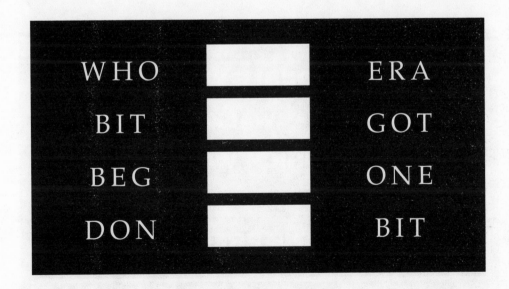

WORD PUZZLE 36

Place two letters in the empty space which, when added to the
end of the words to the left and to the beginning of the right, form
other English words. When this is completed another word
can be read down. What is the word?

ANSWER 37

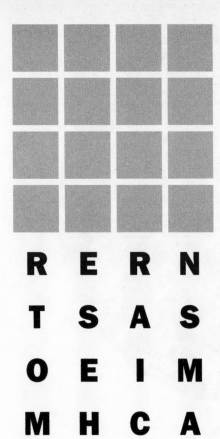

R E R N

T S A S

O E I M

M H C A

WORD PUZZLE 37

Take the letters and arrange them correctly in the column under which they appear. Once this has been done a famous person will appear. Who is the person?

ANSWER 79

AFTER THE DOUBLE WEDDING, THE TWO • • • • • • WALKED THROUGH THE HALL, WHICH WAS LITTERED WITH THE • • • • • • FROM THE PARTY HELD THE PREVIOUS NIGHT.

WORD PUZZLE 38

Two words using the same letters in their construction can be used to replace the dots in this sentence. The sentence will then make sense. Each dot is one letter. What are the words?

ANSWER 27

A P P L E S	6 9
P E A R S	5 9
P E A C H E S	?
M E L O N S	7 8

WORD PUZZLE 39

Here are some fruit.
The number of each is set alongside the
name of the fruit in the diagram.
There is a relationship between the number
and the letters of the names.
How many peaches are there?

ANSWER 69

LADY		WISE
APE		ABLE
GOD		NESS

WORD PUZZLE 40

Place an English word of FOUR letters in the empty space. This
word, when added to the end of the three words to the left and to
the beginning of the three words to the right, will form six other
words. What is the word?

ANSWER 17

WORD PUZZLE 41

Place one letter in the middle of this diagram. Four five-letter
words can now be rearranged from each straight line of letters.
What is the letter and what are the words?

ANSWER 58

WORD PUZZLE 42

Arrange the tiles in this diagram so that they form a square.
When this is done correctly four words can be read downwards
and across. What are the words?

ANSWER 6

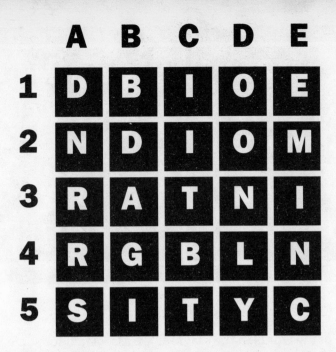

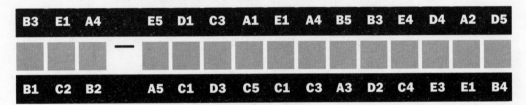

WORD PUZZLE 43

Select one of the two letters from the grid, in accordance with the reference shown, and place it in the word frame. When the correct letters have been chosen a word can be read.
What is the word?

ANSWER 99

WORD PUZZLE 44

Make a circle out of these shapes.
When the correct circle has been found an English word can be read clockwise. What is the word?

ANSWER 47

CARGO	CEDAR
SEDAN	AGAVE
HEDGE	EMBER
DIGIT	MEDAL
PILOT	WEDGE

WORD PUZZLE 45

Five of the words in the diagram are associated for some
reason. Find the words and then work out whether SYRUP belongs
to the group.

ANSWER 88

WORD PUZZLE 46

Move from circle to touching circle collecting the letters of FROG.
Always start at the F.
How many different ways are there to do this?

ANSWER 36

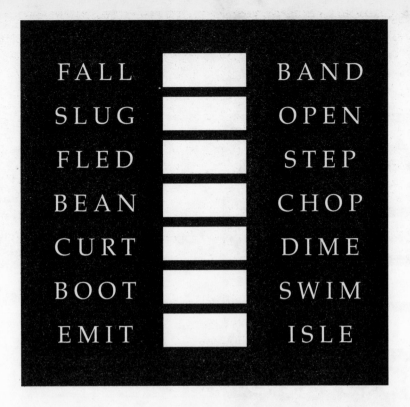

WORD PUZZLE 47

Change the second letter of each word to the left and the right.
Two other English words must be formed. Place the letter used in
the empty section. When this has been completed for all the words
another English word can be read down. What is the word?

ANSWER 78

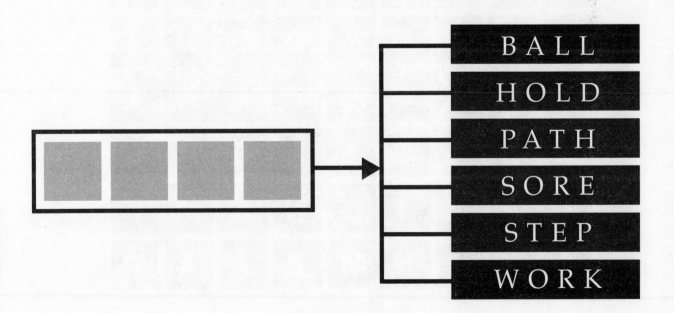

WORD PUZZLE 48

Which English word of four letters can be attached to the front of
the words shown in the diagram to create six other words?

ANSWER 26

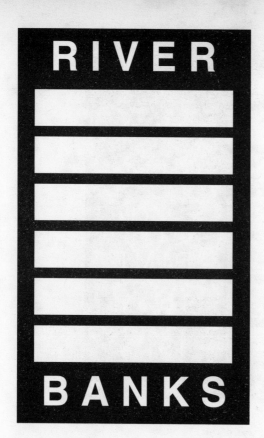

RIVER

BANKS

WORD PUZZLE 49

Complete the word ladder by changing
one letter of each word per step.
The newly created word must be found
in the dictionary.
What are the words to turn
RIVER to BANKS?

ANSWER 68

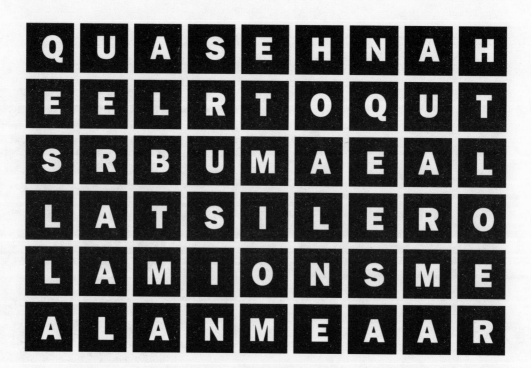

Q	U	A	S	E	H	N	A	H
E	E	L	R	T	O	Q	U	T
S	R	B	U	M	A	E	A	L
L	A	T	S	I	L	E	R	O
L	A	M	I	O	N	S	M	E
A	L	A	N	M	E	A	A	R

WORD PUZZLE 50

A quotation has been written in this diagram. Find the start letter
and move from square to touching square until you have found it.
What is the quotation and to whom is it attributed?

ANSWER 16

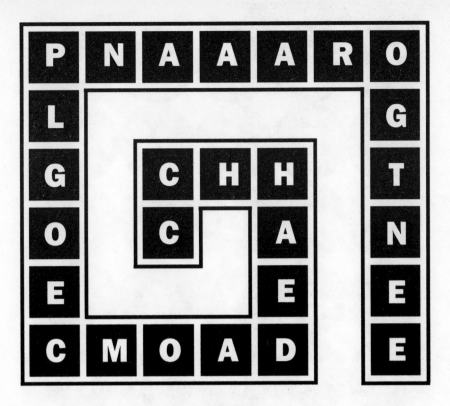

WORD PUZZLE 51

The names of three drinks are to be found in the diagram.
The letters of the names are in the order they normally appear.
What are the drinks?

ANSWER 57

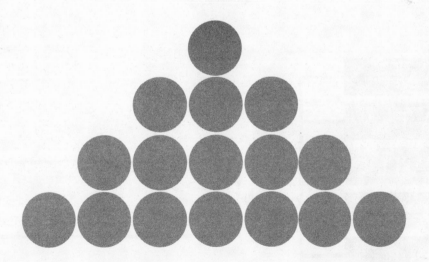

A B C E E E E E G I M O R S V Y

WORD PUZZLE 52

Place the letters shown into the diagram in such a way
that three words can be read across and one down the middle.
What are the words?

ANSWER 5

WORD PUZZLE 53

Start at the letter L and move from circle to touching circle to the H
at the top right. How many different ways are there of collecting
the nine letters of LABYRINTH?

ANSWER 98

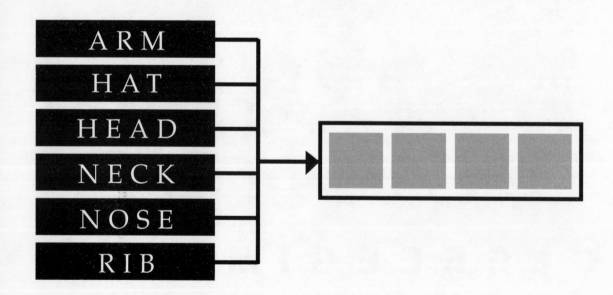

WORD PUZZLE 54

Which English word of four letters can be attached to the back of
the words shown in the diagram to create six other words?

ANSWER 46

WORD PUZZLE 55

Select one letter from each of the segments.
When the correct letters have been found a word of eight letters
can be read clockwise. What is the word?

ANSWER 87

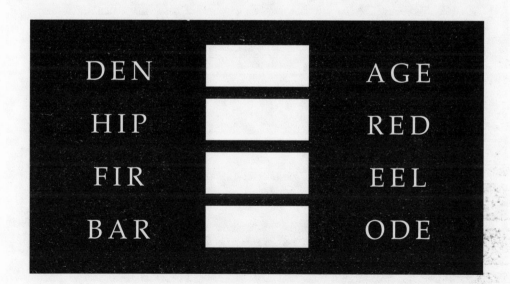

DEN		AGE
HIP		RED
FIR		EEL
BAR		ODE

WORD PUZZLE 56

Place two letters in the empty space which, when added to the
end of the words to the left and to the beginning of the right, form
other English words. When this is completed another word
can be read downwards. What is the word?

ANSWER 35

P H M V
O Y O E
T L W S
E D E H

WORD PUZZLE 57

Take the letters and arrange
them correctly in the column
under which they appear.
Once this has been done a movie
title will appear.
What is the movie?

ANSWER 77

AUSTRALIA	960
MADAGASCAR	1152
IRELAND	576
CUBA	?

WORD PUZZLE 58

The distances on this departure board are fictitious. They bear a
relationship to the letters in the names, What should replace the
question mark ?

ANSWER 25

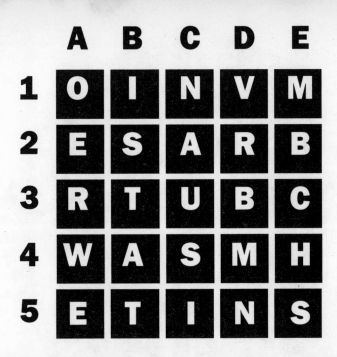

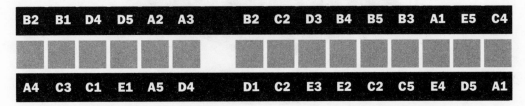

WORD PUZZLE 59

Select one of the two letters from the grid, in accordance with the reference shown, and place it in the word frame. When the correct letters have been chosen two linked words can be read.
What are the words?

ANSWER 67

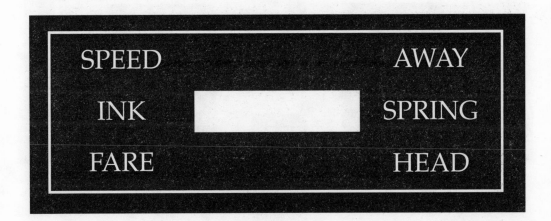

WORD PUZZLE 60

Place an English word of FOUR letters in the empty space. This word, when added to the end of the three words to the left and to the beginning of the three words to the right, will form six other words. What is the word?

ANSWER 15

WORD PUZZLE 61

Place one letter in the middle of this diagram. Four five-letter
words can now be rearranged from each straight line of letters.
What is the letter and what are the words?

ANSWER 56

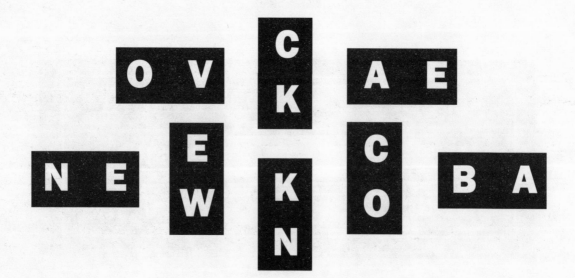

WORD PUZZLE 62

Arrange the tiles in this diagram so that they form a square.
When this is done correctly four words can be read down and
across. What are the words?

ANSWER 4

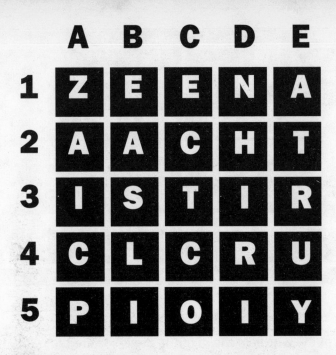

	A	B	C	D	E
1	Z	E	E	N	A
2	A	A	C	H	T
3	I	S	T	I	R
4	C	L	C	R	U
5	P	I	O	I	Y

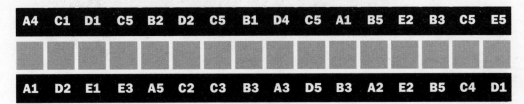

A4	C1	D1	C5	B2	D2	C5	B1	D4	C5	A1	B5	E2	B3	C5	E5
A1	D2	E1	E3	A5	C2	C3	B3	A3	D5	B3	A2	E2	B5	C4	D1

WORD PUZZLE 63

Select one of the two letters from the grid, in accordance with the reference shown, and place it in the word frame. When the correct letters have been chosen a sixteen-letter word can be read. What is the word?

ANSWER 97

WORD PUZZLE 64

Make a circle out of these shapes.
When the correct circle has been found an English word can be read clockwise. What is the word?

ANSWER 45

COYPU	MAYOR
AROMA	BISON
NYMPH	NIGHT
IDYLL	RABBI
BUYER	ABYSS

WORD PUZZLE 65

Five of the words in the diagram are associated for some reason. Find the words and then work out whether STYLE belongs to the group.

ANSWER 86

WORD PUZZLE 66

Move from circle to touching circle collecting the letters of BELL.
Always start at the B.
How many different ways are there to do this?

ANSWER 34

GLOW   BEAT
CONE   DOME
HAVE   MACE
SHOW   ITCH
IRIS   ILEX
READ   LIVE
STAG   SLAB

WORD PUZZLE 67

Change the second letter of each word to the left and the right.
Two other English words must be formed. Place the letter used in
the empty section. When this has been completed for all the words
another English word can be read down. What is the word?

ANSWER 76

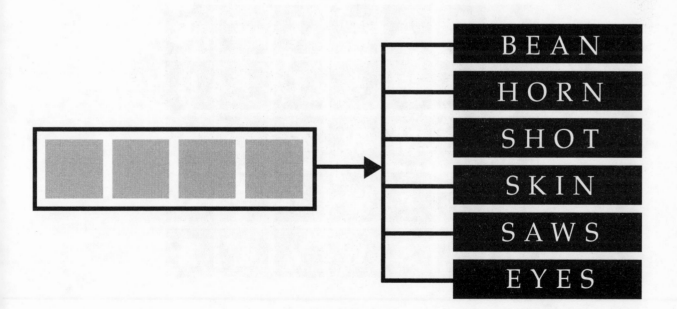

BEAN
HORN
SHOT
SKIN
SAWS
EYES

WORD PUZZLE 68

Which English word of four letters can be attached to the front of
the words shown in the diagram to create six other words?

ANSWER 24

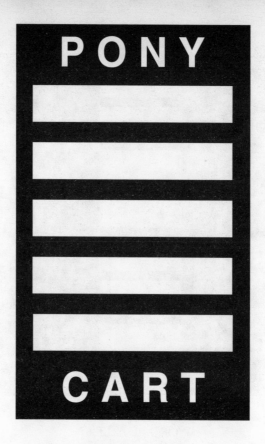

PONY

CART

WORD PUZZLE 69

Complete the word ladder by changing one letter of each word
per step. The newly created word must be found in the dictionary.
What are the words to turn PONY to CART?

ANSWER 66

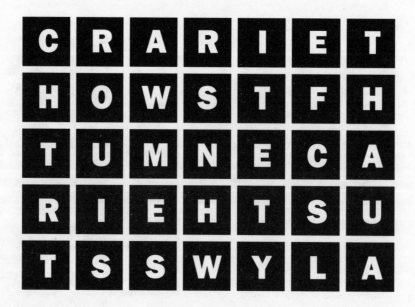

C	R	A	R	I	E	T
H	O	W	S	T	F	H
T	U	M	N	E	C	A
R	I	E	H	T	S	U
T	S	S	W	Y	L	A

WORD PUZZLE 70

A quotation has been written in this diagram. Find the start letter
and move from square to touching square until you have found it.
What is the quotation and to whom is it attributed?

ANSWER 14

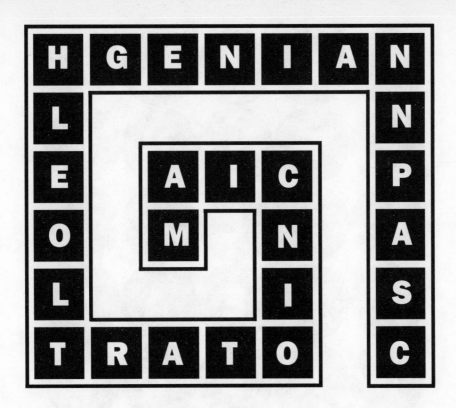

WORD PUZZLE 71

The names of three foods are to be found in the diagram.
The letters of the names are in the order they normally appear.
What are the foods?

ANSWER 55

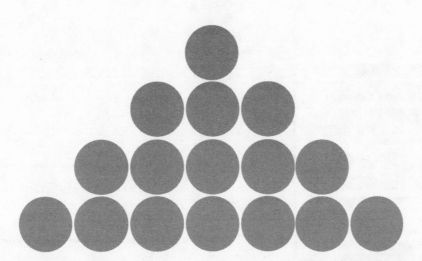

ABDEEEJKLLMNOTWW

WORD PUZZLE 72

Place the letters shown into the diagram in such a way
that three words can be read across and one down the middle.
What are the words?

ANSWER 3

WORD PUZZLE 73

Start at the letter B and move from circle to touching circle to the A
at the top right. How many different ways are there of collecting
the nine letters of BALLERINA?

ANSWER 96

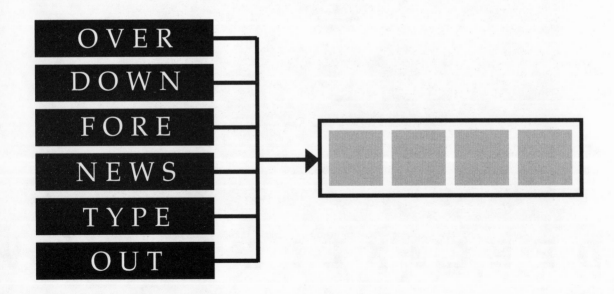

WORD PUZZLE 74

Which English word of four letters can be attached to the back of
the words shown in the diagram to create six other words?

ANSWER 44

WORD PUZZLE 75

Select one letter from each of the segments.
When the correct letters have been found a word of eight letters
can be read clockwise. What is the word?

ANSWER 85

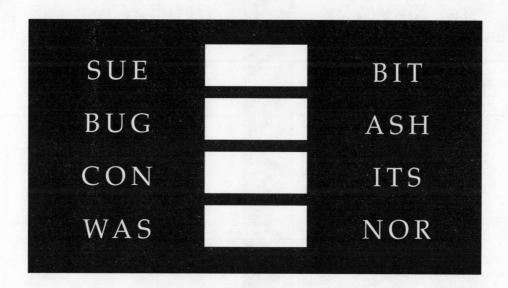

SUE		BIT
BUG		ASH
CON		ITS
WAS		NOR

WORD PUZZLE 76

Place two letters in the empty space which, when added to the
end of the words to the left and to the beginning of the right, form
other English words. When this is completed another word
can be read down. What is the word?

ANSWER 33

T A W S

E V E I

L S N O

D H W C

WORD PUZZLE 77

Take the letters and arrange them correctly in the column under which they appear. Once this has been done a movie title will appear. What is the movie?

ANSWER 75

16 NEWARK   CHICAGO ?

20 PORTLAND   CHARLESTON 26

WORD PUZZLE 78

This is a meaningless signpost but there is a twisted form of logic behind the figures. Discover the logic and find the distance to Chicago. How far is it?

ANSWER 65

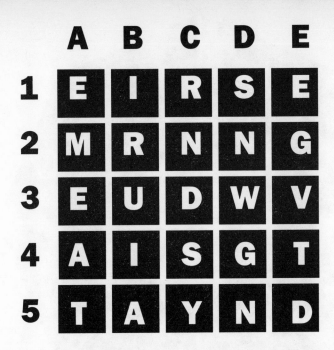

A2 B1 A1 A3 D5 E5 D2 C1 B5 A5 A4 D3 E1 B4 E1 D4

C4 A5 C4 B3 B2 B1 E1 E2 D1 D5 C5 C2 C3 E3 D2 E4

WORD PUZZLE 79

Select one of the two letters from the grid, in accordance with the reference shown, and place it in the word frame. When the correct letters have been chosen a sixteen-letter word can be read. What is the word?

ANSWER 23

BELL   MAN

BLUE   [ ]   BATH

JAIL   LIME

WORD PUZZLE 80

Place an English word of FOUR letters in the empty space. This word, when added to the end of the three words to the left and to the beginning of the three words to the right, will form six other words. What is the word?

ANSWER 13

WORD PUZZLE 81

Place one letter in the middle of this diagram. Four five-letter
words can now be rearranged from each straight line of letters.
What is the letter and what are the words?

ANSWER 54

WORD PUZZLE 82

Arrange the tiles in this diagram so that they form a square.
When this is done correctly four words can be read down and
across. What are the words?

ANSWER 2

	A	B	C	D	E
1	F	U	R	C	N
2	I	A	T	Q	I
3	N	I	O	I	T
4	I	Y	S	A	L
5	C	A	K	L	D

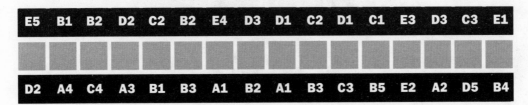

| E5 | B1 | B2 | D2 | C2 | B2 | E4 | D3 | D1 | C2 | D1 | C1 | E3 | D3 | C3 | E1 |

| D2 | A4 | C4 | A3 | B1 | B3 | A1 | B2 | A1 | B3 | C3 | B5 | E2 | A2 | D5 | B4 |

WORD PUZZLE 83

Select one of the two letters from the grid, in accordance with the reference shown, and place it in the word frame. When the correct letters have been chosen a sixteen-letter word can be read. What is the word?

ANSWER 95

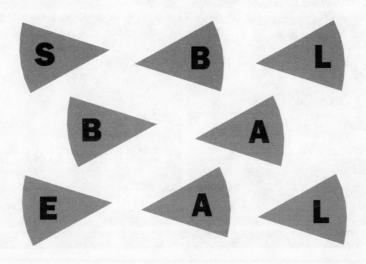

WORD PUZZLE 84

Make a circle out of these shapes.
When the correct circle has been found an English word can be read clockwise. What is the word?

ANSWER 43

WORD PUZZLE 85

Move from circle to touching circle collecting the letters of SILK.
Always start at the S.
How many different ways are there to do this?

ANSWER 84

EPOCH	TULIP
SWINE	EXILE
OKAPI	ABBEY
DECOY	HIPPO
STEAM	BLOND

WORD PUZZLE 86

Five of the words in the diagram are associated for some
reason. Find the words and then work out whether FLUTE belongs
to the group.

ANSWER 32

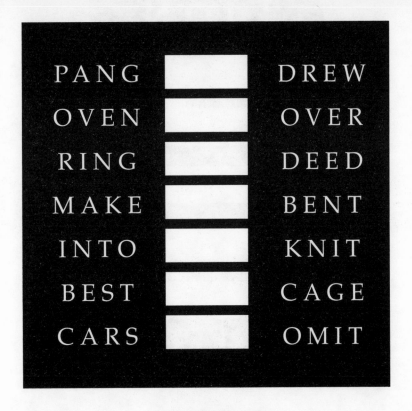

PANG		DREW
OVEN		OVER
RING		DEED
MAKE		BENT
INTO		KNIT
BEST		CAGE
CARS		OMIT

WORD PUZZLE 87

Change the first letter of each word to the left and the right. Two other English words must be formed. Place the letter used in the empty section. When this has been completed for all the words another English word can be read downwards. What is the word?

ANSWER 74

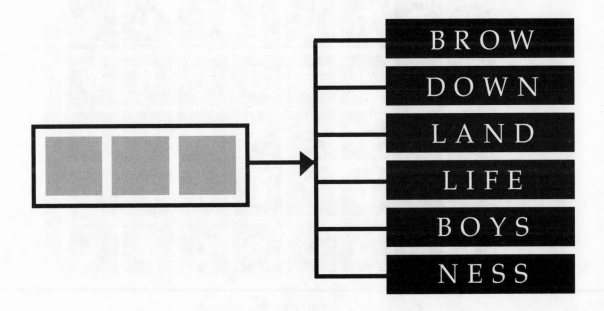

| BROW |
| DOWN |
| LAND |
| LIFE |
| BOYS |
| NESS |

WORD PUZZLE 88

Which English word of three letters can be attached to the front of the words shown in the diagram to create six other words?

ANSWER 22

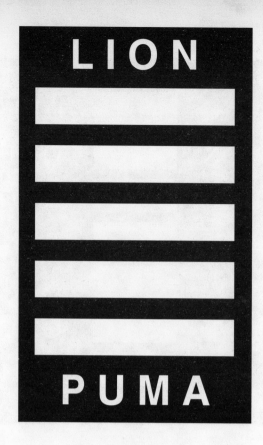

LION

PUMA

WORD PUZZLE 89

Complete the word ladder by changing one letter of each word per step. The newly created word must be found in the dictionary. What are the words to turn LION to PUMA?

ANSWER 64

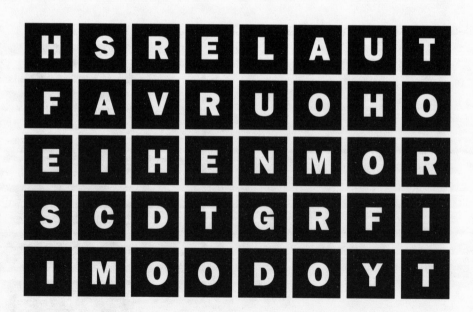

H	S	R	E	L	A	U	T
F	A	V	R	U	O	H	O
E	I	H	E	N	M	O	R
S	C	D	T	G	R	F	I
I	M	O	O	D	O	Y	T

WORD PUZZLE 90

A quotation has been written in this diagram. Find the start letter and move from square to touching square until you have found it. What is the quotation and to whom is it attributed?

ANSWER 12

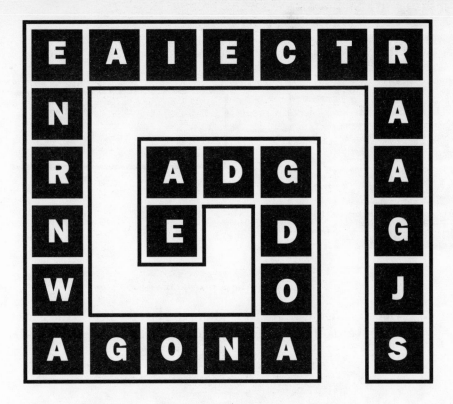

WORD PUZZLE 91

The names of three trees are to be found in the diagram.
The letters of the names are in the order they normally appear.
What are the trees?

ANSWER 53

CDEHMNOOOOPPRSST

WORD PUZZLE 92

Place the letters shown into the diagram in such a way
that three words can be read across and one down the middle.
What are the words?

ANSWER 1

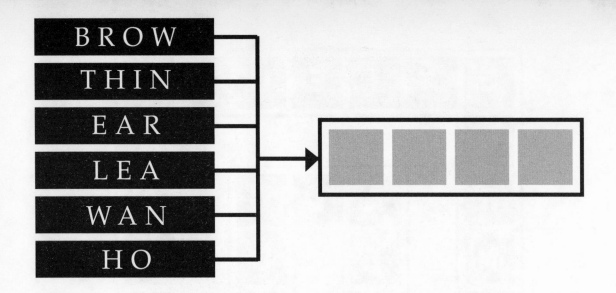

BROW
THIN
EAR
LEA
WAN
HO

WORD PUZZLE 93

Which English word of four letters can be attached to the back of
the words shown in the diagram to create six other words?

ANSWER 42

G I N O E
R I G I N
R O I G I
B O R I G
A B O R I

WORD PUZZLE 94

Start at the bottom letter A and move from circle to touching circle
to the E at the top right. How many different ways are there of
collecting the nine letters of ABORIGINE?

ANSWER 94

WORD PUZZLE 95

Select one letter from each of the segments.
When the correct letters have been found a word of eight letters
can be read clockwise. What is the word?

ANSWER 83

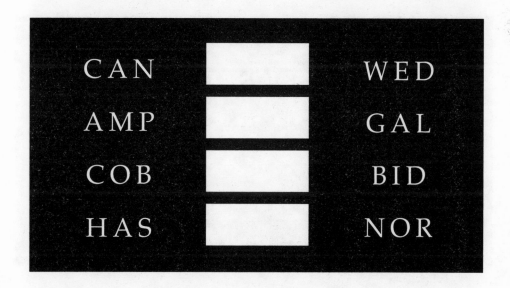

CAN		WED
AMP		GAL
COB		BID
HAS		NOR

WORD PUZZLE 96

Place two letters in the empty space which, when added to the
end of the words to the left and to the beginning of the right, form
other English words. When this is completed another word
can be read down. What is the word?

ANSWER 31

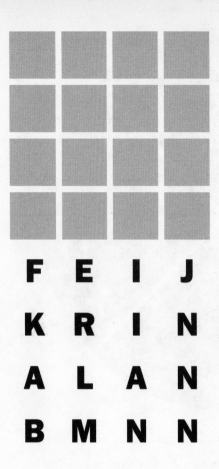

F E I J

K R I N

A L A N

B M N N

WORD PUZZLE 97

Take the letters and arrange
them correctly in the column
under which they appear.
Once this has been done a famous
person will appear.
Who is the person?

ANSWER 73

THE PROFESSIONAL WRESTLER

WAS OF • • • • • • BUILD AND

BORE A • • • • • • AGAINST

HIS OPPONENT.

WORD PUZZLE 98

Two words using the same letters in their construction can be used
to replace the dots in this sentence. The sentence will then make
sense. Each dot is one letter. What are the words?

ANSWER 21

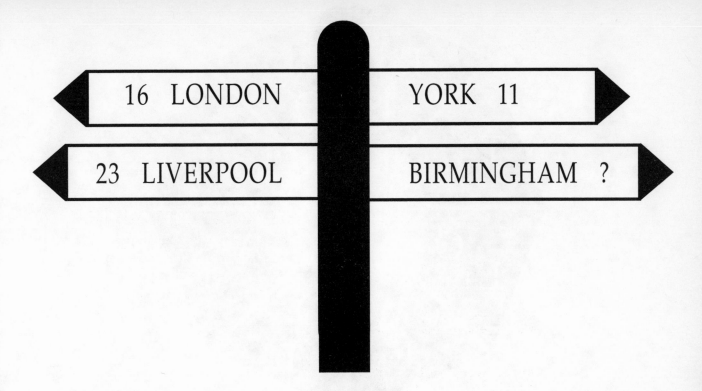

WORD PUZZLE 99

The distances on this signpost are fictitious. They bear a relationship to the letters in the names.
What should replace the question mark?

ANSWER 63

WORD PUZZLE 100

Place an English word of FOUR letters in the empty space. This
word, when added to the end of the three words to the left and to
the beginning of the three words to the right, will form six other
words. What is the word?

ANSWER 11

WORD PUZZLE 101

Place one letter in the middle of this diagram. Four five-letter
words can now be rearranged from each straight line of letters.
What is the letter and what are the words?

ANSWER 52

WORD PUZZLE 102

Arrange the tiles in this diagram so that they form a square.
When this is done correctly five words can be read downwards
and across. What are the words?

ANSWER 104

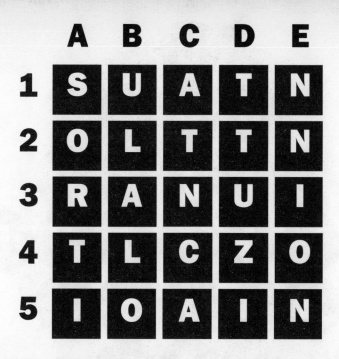

	A	B	C	D	E
1	S	U	A	T	N
2	O	L	T	T	N
3	R	A	N	U	I
4	T	L	C	Z	O
5	I	O	A	I	N

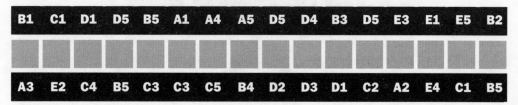

B1	C1	D1	D5	B5	A1	A4	A5	D5	D4	B3	D5	E3	E1	E5	B2
A3	E2	C4	B5	C3	C3	C5	B4	D2	D3	D1	C2	A2	E4	C1	B5

WORD PUZZLE 103

Select one of the two letters from the grid, in accordance with the reference shown, and place it in the word frame. When the correct letters have been chosen a sixteen-letter word can be read. What is the word?

ANSWER 93

WORD PUZZLE 104

Make a circle out of these shapes.
When the correct circle has been found an English word can be read clockwise. What is the word?

ANSWER 41

WORD PUZZLE 105

Move from circle to touching circle collecting the letters of FISH.
Always start at the F.
How many different ways are there to do this?

ANSWER 167

ASPIC	IMAGE
STEEL	ANNOY
LEAFY	COMMA
JETTY	AGENT
BEACH	CADDY

WORD PUZZLE 106

Five of the words in the diagram are associated for some
reason. Find the words and then work out whether CHEER
belongs to the group.

ANSWER 115

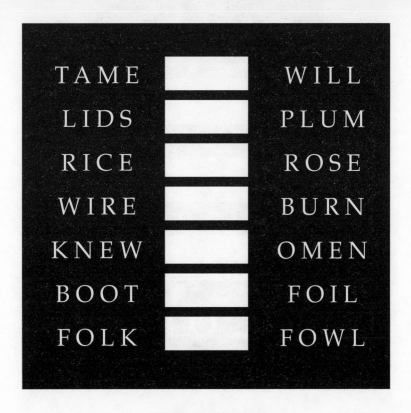

TAME		WILL
LIDS		PLUM
RICE		ROSE
WIRE		BURN
KNEW		OMEN
BOOT		FOIL
FOLK		FOWL

WORD PUZZLE 107

Change the first letter of each word to the left and the right. Two other English words must be formed. Place the letter used in the empty section. When this has been completed for all the words another English word can be read down. What is the word?

ANSWER 134

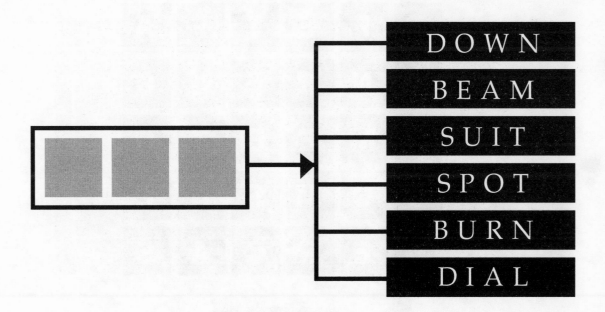

DOWN
BEAM
SUIT
SPOT
BURN
DIAL

WORD PUZZLE 108

Which English word of three letters can be attached to the front of the words shown in the diagram to create six other words?

ANSWER 156

WORD PUZZLE 109

Complete the word ladder by changing one letter of each word
per step. The newly created word must be found in the dictionary.
What are the words to turn BLAZE to GLORY?

ANSWER 197

WORD PUZZLE 110

A quotation has been written in this diagram. Find the start letter
and move from square to touching square until you have found it.
What is the quotation and to whom is it attributed?

ANSWER 145

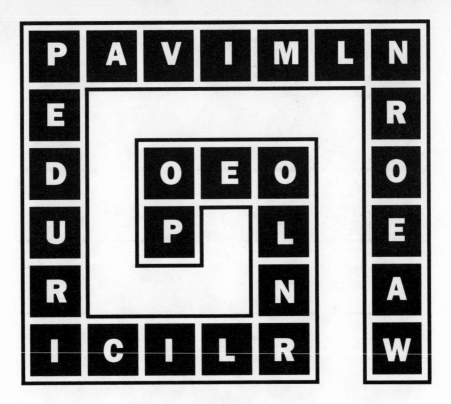

WORD PUZZLE 111

The names of three animals are to be found in the diagram.
The letters of the names are in the order they normally appear.
What are the animals?

ANSWER 166

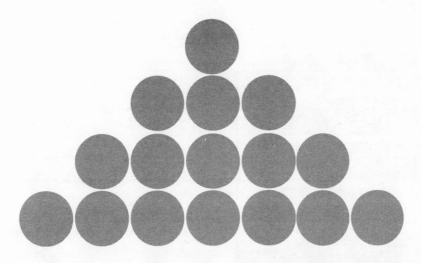

A A A E E I M M N N N O R R S T

WORD PUZZLE 112

Place the letters shown into the diagram in such a way
that three words can be read across and one down the middle.
What are the words?

ANSWER 114

WORD PUZZLE 113

Start at the bottom letter F and move from circle to touching circle
to the S at the top right. How many different ways are there of collecting the nine letters of FESTIVALS ?

ANSWER 125

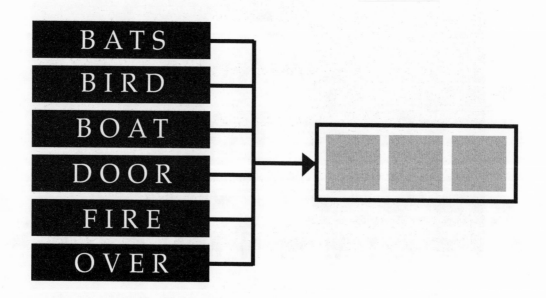

WORD PUZZLE 114

Which English word of three letters can be attached to the back of
the words shown in the diagram to create six other words?

ANSWER 155

WORD PUZZLE 115

Select one letter from each of the segments.
When the correct letters have been found a word of eight letters
can be read clockwise. What is the word?

ANSWER 196

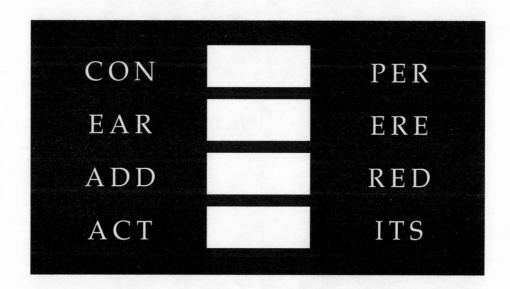

CON		PER
EAR		ERE
ADD		RED
ACT		ITS

WORD PUZZLE 116

Place two letters in the empty space which, when added to the
end of the words to the left and to the beginning of the right, form
other English words. When this is completed another word
can be read down. What is the word?

ANSWER 144

```
H  O  R  C
T  I  N  S
W  U  L  L
H  I  N  C
```

WORD PUZZLE 117

Take the letters and arrange
them correctly in the column
under which they appear.
Once this has been done the name
of a famous person will emerge.
What is the name ?

ANSWER 186

WORD PUZZLE 118

Start at the bottom letter M and move from circle to touching circle
to the S at the top right. How many different ways are there of
collecting the nine letters of MAGAZINES?

ANSWER 177

PIZZA	78
BURGER	71
STEAK	56
FRIES	?

WORD PUZZLE 119

On this list of stock the number of packets of each food are written
. The numbers bear a relationship to the letters in the words. What
should replace the question mark?

ANSWER 176

ADD		PAPER
IMP	END	LESS
LEG		EAR

WORD PUZZLE 120

Place an English word of THREE letters in the empty space. This
word, when added to the end of the three words to the left and to
the beginning of the three words to the right, will form six other
words. What is the word?

ANSWER 124

WORD PUZZLE 121

Place one letter in the middle of this diagram. Four five-letter
words can now be rearranged from each straight line of letters.
What is the letter and what are the words?

ANSWER 165

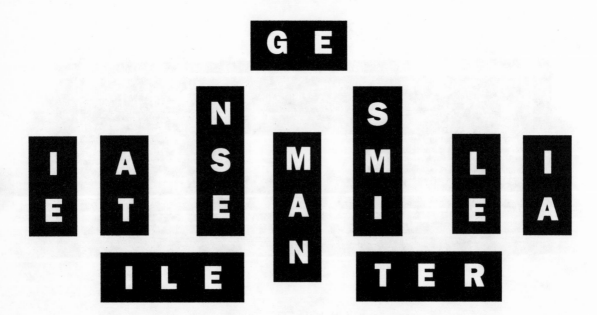

WORD PUZZLE 122

Arrange the tiles in this diagram so that they form a square.
When this is done correctly five words can be read downwards
and across. What are the words?

ANSWER 113

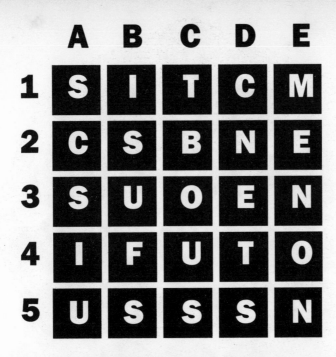

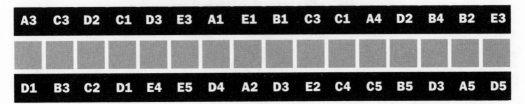

WORD PUZZLE 123

Select one of the two letters from the grid, in accordance with the
reference shown, and place it in the word frame. When the correct
letters have been chosen a sixteen-letter word can be read.
What is the word?

ANSWER 206

WORD PUZZLE 124

Make a circle out of these shapes.
When the correct circle has been found an English word can be
read clockwise. What is the word?

ANSWER 154

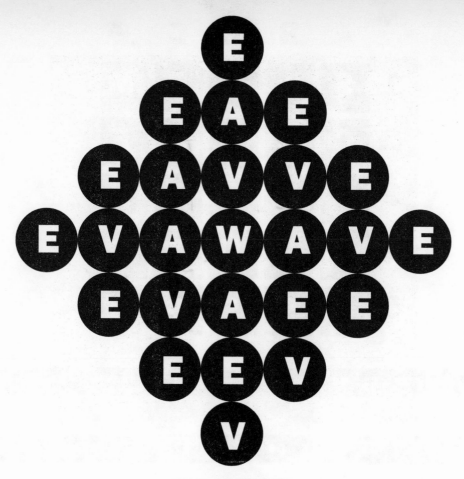

WORD PUZZLE 125

Move from circle to touching circle collecting the letters of WAVE.
Always start at the W.
How many different ways are there to do this?

ANSWER 195

BACON   BABES

GAMES   GIPSY

SUSHI   RESIN

PAPER   TALES

TRAIN   CAKES

WORD PUZZLE 126

Five of the words in the diagram are associated for some
reason. Find the words and then work out whether CAFES belongs
to the group.

ANSWER 143

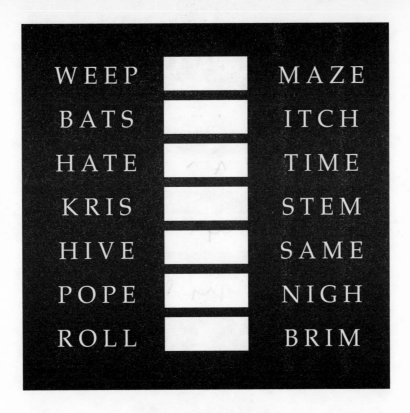

WORD PUZZLE 127

Change the first letter of each word to the left and the right. Two
other English words must be formed. Place the letter used in the
empty section. When this has been completed for all the words
another English word can be read down. What is the word?

ANSWER 185

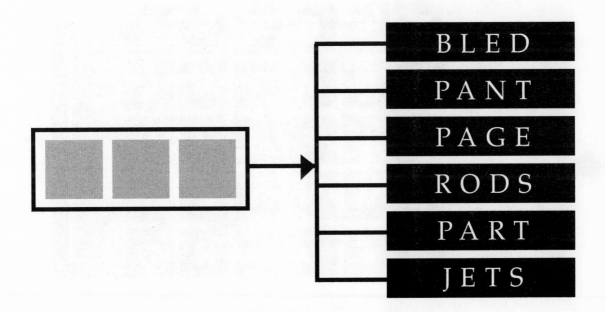

WORD PUZZLE 128

Which English word of three letters can be attached to the front of
the words shown in the diagram to create six other words?

ANSWER 133

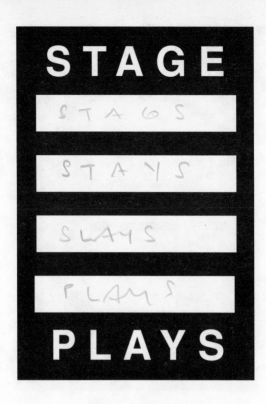

STAGE

STAGS

STAYS

SLAYS

PLAYS

PLAYS

WORD PUZZLE 129

Complete the word ladder by changing one letter of each word
per step. The newly created word must be found in the dictionary.
What are the words to turn STAGE to PLAYS?

ANSWER 175

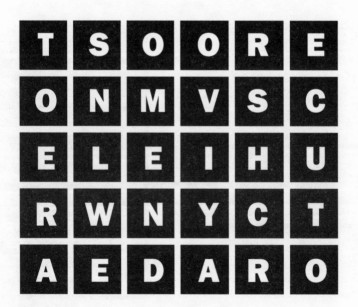

T	S	O	O	R	E
O	N	M	V	S	C
E	L	E	I	H	U
R	W	N	Y	C	T
A	E	D	A	R	O

WORD PUZZLE 130

A quotation has been written in this diagram. Find the start letter
and move from square to touching square until you have found it.
What is the quotation and to whom is it attributed?

ANSWER 123

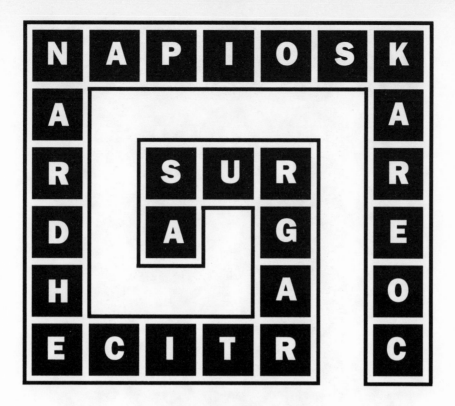

WORD PUZZLE 131

The names of three plants are to be found in the diagram.
The letters of the names are in the order they normally appear.
What are theplants?

ANSWER 164

IN THE FOREST AS THE

FRUIT • • • • • • THE

FURTIVE • • • • • • LURKS

IN ANTICIPATION OF

HIS VICTIM.

WORD PUZZLE 132

Two words using the same letters in their construction can be used
to replace the dots in this sentence. The sentence will then make
sense. Each dot is one letter. What are the words?

ANSWER 112

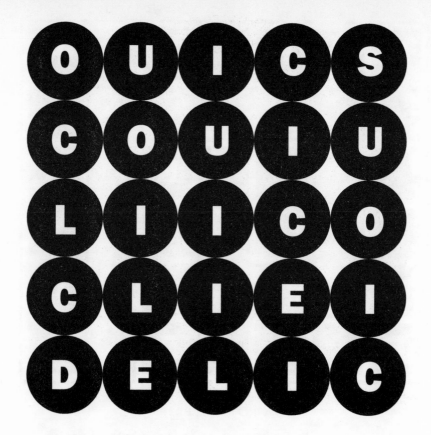

WORD PUZZLE 133

Start at the bottom letter D and move from circle to touching circle
to the S at the top right. How many different ways are there of collecting the nine letters of DELICIOUS?

ANSWER 205

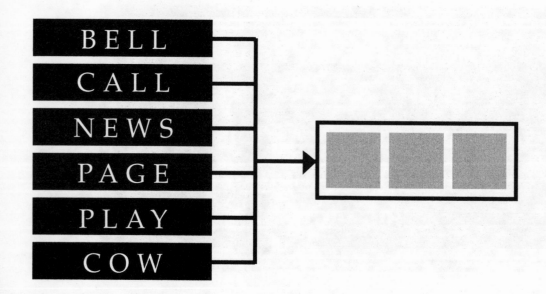

WORD PUZZLE 134

Which English word of three letters can be attached to the back of
the words shown in the diagram to create six other words?

ANSWER 153

WORD PUZZLE 135

Select one letter from each of the segments.
When the correct letters have been found a word of eight letters
can be read clockwise. What is the word?

ANSWER 194

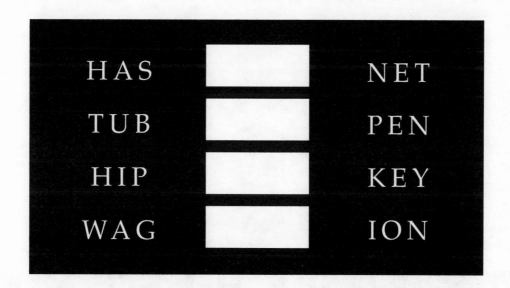

HAS		NET
TUB		PEN
HIP		KEY
WAG		ION

WORD PUZZLE 136

Place two letters in the empty space which, when added to the
end of the words to the left and to the beginning of the right, form
other English words.
When this is completed another word can be read down. What is
the word?

ANSWER 142

S E O N

G H O R

G T W A

G E I N

WORD PUZZLE 137

Take the letters and arrange
them correctly in the column
under which they appear.
Once this has been done the name
of a famous person will emerge.
What is the name?

ANSWER 184

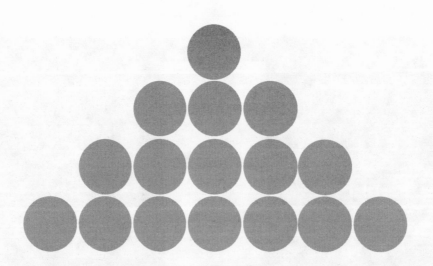

A A A B C D D E H I K L M N R Y

WORD PUZZLE 138

Place the letters shown into the diagram in such a way
that three words can be read across and one down the middle.
What are the words?

ANSWER 132

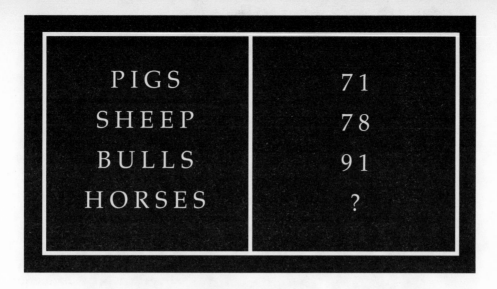

WORD PUZZLE 139

On this list of farm stock the number of animals is written. The
numbers bear a relationship to the letters in the words. What
should replace the question mark?

ANSWER 174

WORD PUZZLE 140

Place an English word of THREE letters in the empty space.
This word, when added to the end of the three words to the left
and to the beginning of the three words to the right, will form six
other words. What is the word?

ANSWER 122

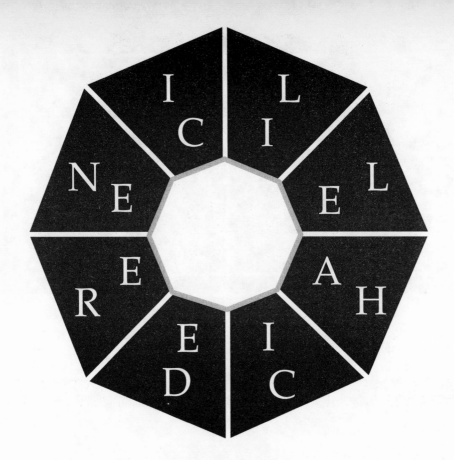

WORD PUZZLE 141

Place one letter in the middle of this diagram. Four five-letter
words can now be rearranged from each straight line of letters.
What is the letter and what are the words?

ANSWER 163

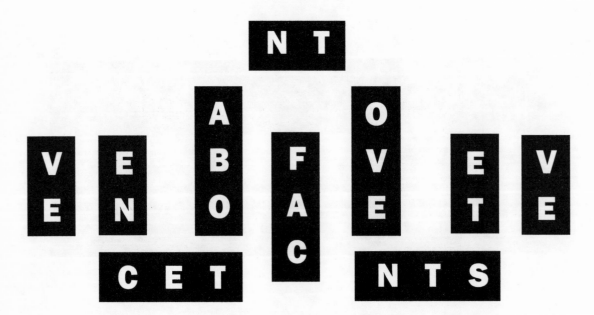

WORD PUZZLE 142

Arrange the tiles in this diagram so that they form a square.
When this is done correctly five words can be read down and
across. What are the words?

ANSWER 111

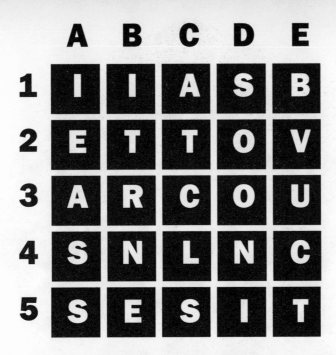

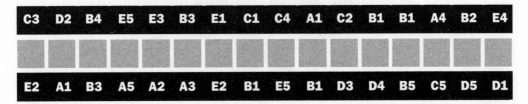

| C3 | D2 | B4 | E5 | E3 | B3 | E1 | C1 | C4 | A1 | C2 | B1 | B1 | A4 | B2 | E4 |

| E2 | A1 | B3 | A5 | A2 | A3 | E2 | B1 | E5 | B1 | D3 | D4 | B5 | C5 | D5 | D1 |

WORD PUZZLE 143

Select one of the two letters from the grid, in accordance with the
reference shown, and place it in the word frame. When the correct
letters have been chosen a sixteen-letter word can be read.
What is the word?

ANSWER 204

WORD PUZZLE 144

Make a circle out of these shapes.
When the correct circle has been found an English word can be
read clockwise. What is the word?

ANSWER 152

WORD PUZZLE 145

Move from circle to touching circle collecting the letters of BOAT.
Always start at the B.
How many different ways are there to do this?

ANSWER 193

STAGE	BREAD
TUTOR	DREAD
COMIC	YUCCA
LOYAL	ARENA
SAUNA	KIOSK

WORD PUZZLE 146

Five of the words in the diagram are associated for some
reason. Find the words and then work out whether WIDOW
belongs to the group.

ANSWER 141

THIN		RAGE
SKIN		FIRS
WIFE		BUMP
SOUR		TANK
DARK		MOST
CHIP		WEAR
WILY		BATH

WORD PUZZLE 147

Change the first letter of each word to the left and the right. Two other English words must be formed. Place the letter used in the empty section. When this has been completed for all the words another English word can be read down. What is the word?

ANSWER 183

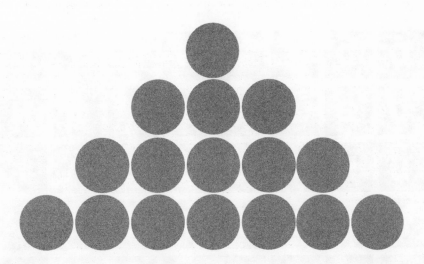

A A A B C E E E H M M M R T T Z

WORD PUZZLE 148

Place the letters shown into the diagram in such a way that three words can be read across and one down the middle. What are the words?

ANSWER 131

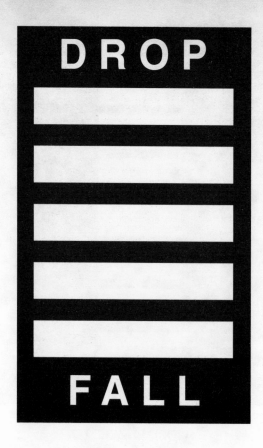

WORD PUZZLE 149

Complete the word ladder by changing one letter of each word per step. The newly created word must be found in the dictionary. What are the words to turn DROP to FALL?

ANSWER 173

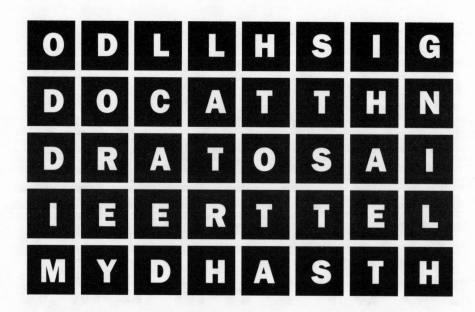

WORD PUZZLE 150

A quotation has been written in this diagram. Find the start letter and move from square to touching square until you have found it. What is the quotation and to whom is it attributed?

ANSWER 121

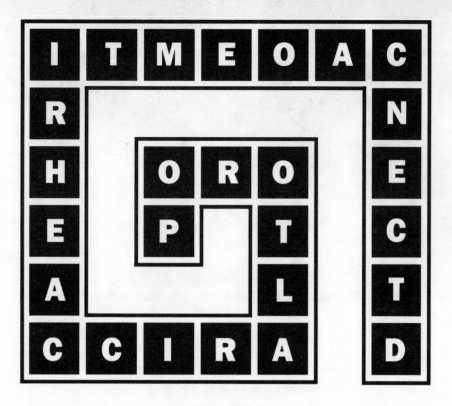

WORD PUZZLE 151

The names of three professions are to be found in the diagram.
The letters of the names are in the order they normally appear.
What are the professions?

ANSWER 162

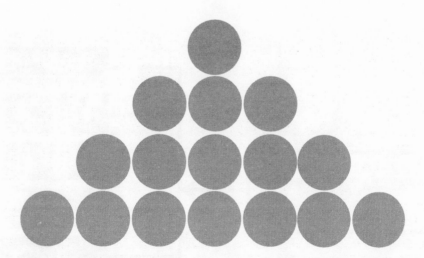

A B C C C H I I N O O S T T T U

WORD PUZZLE 152

Place the letters shown into the diagram in such a way
that three words can be read across and one down the middle.
What are the words?

ANSWER 110

THE VALUABLE SCIENTIFIC EQUIPMENT WAS CAREFULLY ● ● ● ● ● ● AND CHECKED BEFORE BEING ● ● ● ● ● ● TO THE OTHER SIDE OF THE BUILDING.

WORD PUZZLE 153

Two words using the same letters in their construction can be used to replace the dots in this sentence. The sentence will then make sense. Each dot is one letter. What are the words?

ANSWER 203

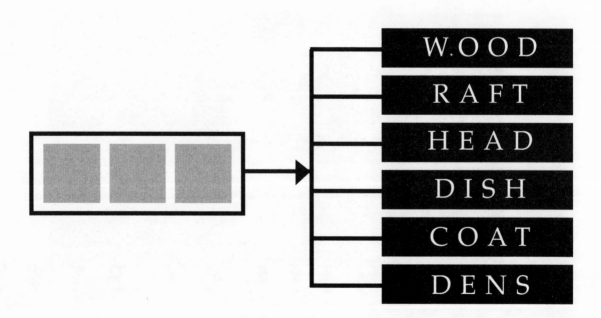

WORD PUZZLE 154

Which English word of three letters can be attached to the front of the words shown in the diagram to create six other words?

ANSWER 151

WORD PUZZLE 155

Select one letter from each of the segments.
When the correct letters have been found a word of eight letters
can be read clockwise. What is the word?

ANSWER 192

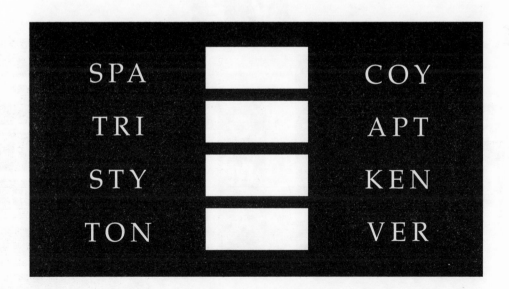

WORD PUZZLE 156

Place two letters in the empty space which, when added to the
end of the words to the left and to the beginning of the right, form
other English words. When this is completed another word
can be read down. What is the word?

ANSWER 140

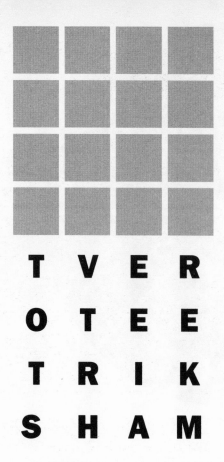

T V E R
O T E E
T R I K
S H A M

WORD PUZZLE 157

Take the letters and arrange them correctly in the column under which they appear. Once this has been done the name of a film will emerge. What is it?

ANSWER 182

WORD PUZZLE 158

Arrange the tiles in this diagram so that they form a square. When this is done correctly five words can be read down and across. What are the words?

ANSWER 130

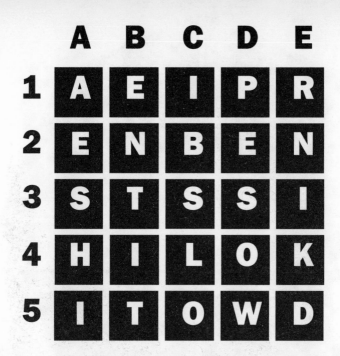

	A	B	C	D	E
1	A	E	I	P	R
2	E	N	B	E	N
3	S	T	S	S	I
4	H	I	L	O	K
5	I	T	O	W	D

E1	A1	E1	B1	D4	B3	A3	A5	D4	E5	C4	E1	D5	D4	D2	E4
D1	A2	C3	D1	B2	E2	A4	C5	C2	C1	D4	B4	B5	E3	E1	D3

WORD PUZZLE 159

Select one of the two letters from the grid, in accordance with the
reference shown, and place it in the word frame. When the correct
letters have been chosen a sixteen-letter word can be read.
What is the word?

ANSWER 172

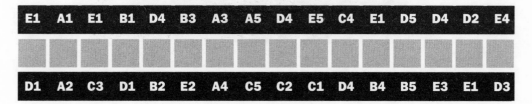

THE LANGUAGE USED BY THE
• • • • • • AT THE BASEBALL GAME
WAS SO • • • • • • IT WAS
SCARCELY UNDERSTANDABLE.

WORD PUZZLE 160

Two words using the same letters in their construction can be used
to replace the dots in this sentence. The sentence will then make
sense. Each dot is one letter. What are the words?

ANSWER 120

WORD PUZZLE 161

Place one letter in the middle of this diagram. Four five-letter
words can now be rearranged from each straight line of letters.
What is the letter and what are the words?

ANSWER 161

WORD PUZZLE 162

Arrange the tiles in this diagram so that they form a square.
When this is done correctly five words can be read downwards
and across. What are the words?

ANSWER 109

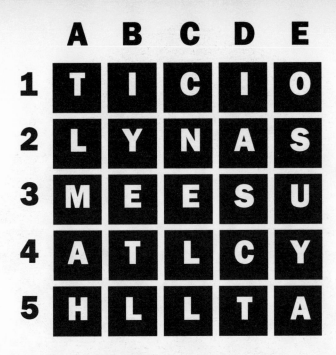

	A	B	C	D	E
1	T	I	C	I	O
2	L	Y	N	A	S
3	M	E	E	S	U
4	A	T	L	C	Y
5	H	L	L	T	A

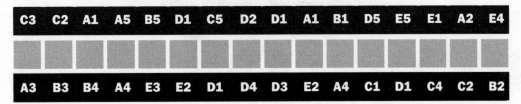

C3	C2	A1	A5	B5	D1	C5	D2	D1	A1	B1	D5	E5	E1	A2	E4
A3	B3	B4	A4	E3	E2	D1	D4	D3	E2	A4	C1	D1	C4	C2	B2

WORD PUZZLE 163

Select one of the two letters from the grid, in accordance with the reference shown, and place it in the word frame. When the correct letters have been chosen a sixteen-letter word can be read.
What is the word?

ANSWER 202

WORD PUZZLE 164

Make a circle out of these shapes.
When the correct circle has been found an English word can be read clockwise. What is the word?

ANSWER 150

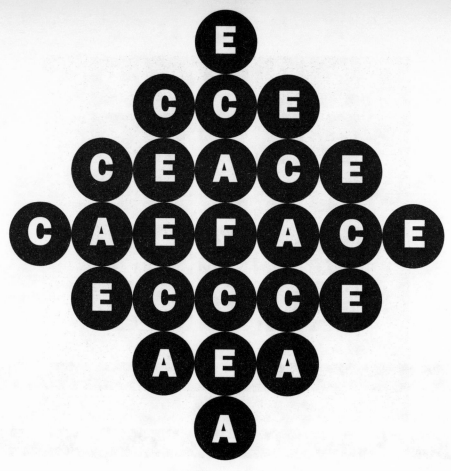

WORD PUZZLE 165

Move from circle to touching circle collecting the letters of FACE.
Always start at the F.
How many different ways are there to do this?

ANSWER 191

HYMNS

SHRUB

PIZZA

ANKLE

PASTA

LIGHT

FILMS

QUEEN

FLAME

INDEX

WORD PUZZLE 166

Six of the words in the diagram are associated for some
reason. Find the words and then work out whether GLOBE
belongs to the group.

ANSWER 139

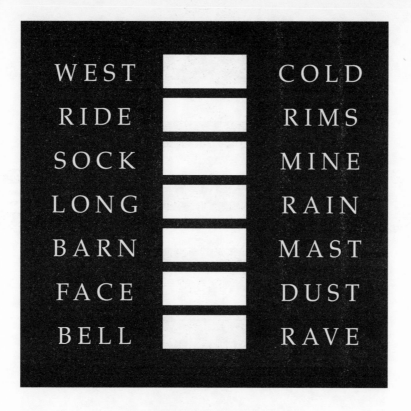

WEST		COLD
RIDE		RIMS
SOCK		MINE
LONG		RAIN
BARN		MAST
FACE		DUST
BELL		RAVE

WORD PUZZLE 167

Change the first letter of each word to the left and the right. Two other English words must be formed. Place the letter used in the empty section. When this has been completed for all the words another English word can be read down. What is the word?

ANSWER 181

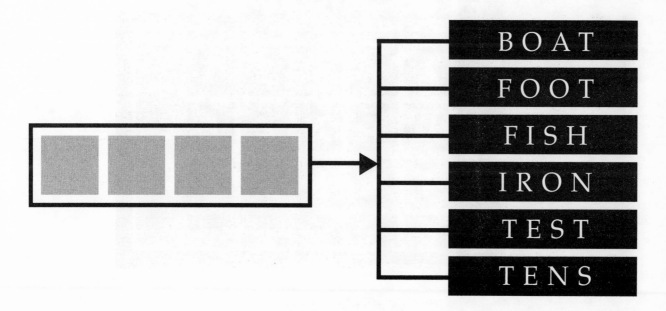

WORD PUZZLE 168

Which English word of four letters can be attached to the front of the words shown in the diagram to create six other words?

ANSWER 129

PORT

SHIP

WORD PUZZLE 169

Complete the word ladder by changing one letter of each word
per step. The newly created word must be found in the dictionary.
What are the words to turn PORT to SHIP?

ANSWER 171

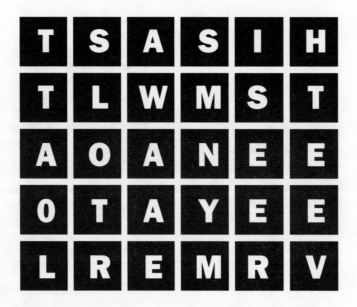

T	S	A	S	I	H
T	L	W	M	S	T
A	O	A	N	E	E
O	T	A	Y	E	E
L	R	E	M	R	V

WORD PUZZLE 170

A quotation has been written in this diagram. Find the start letter
and move from square to touching square until you have found it.
What is the quotation and to whom is it attributed?

ANSWER 119

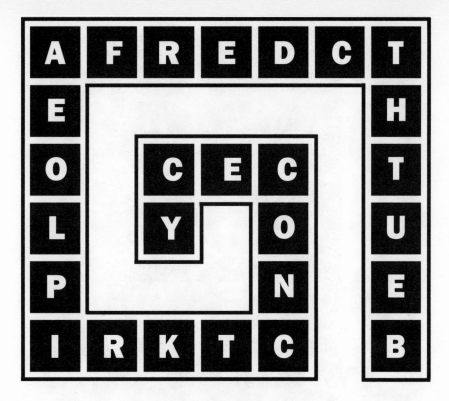

WORD PUZZLE 171

The names of three insects are to be found in the diagram.
The letters of the names are in the order they normally appear.
What are the insects?

ANSWER 160

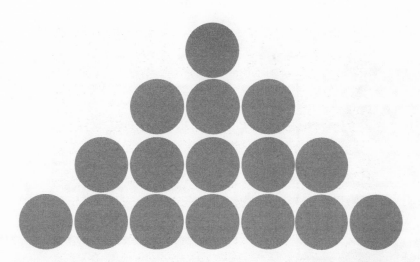

A A A B C C E H N N O O R S S T

WORD PUZZLE 172

Place the letters shown into the diagram in such a way
that three words can be read across and one down the middle.
What are the words?

ANSWER 108

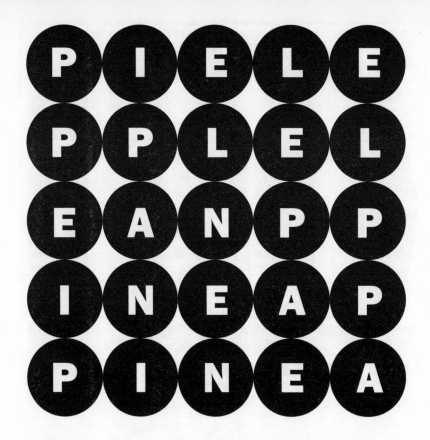

WORD PUZZLE 173

Start at the bottom letter P and move from circle to touching circle to the E at the top right. How many different ways are there of collecting the nine letters of PINEAPPLE?

ANSWER 201

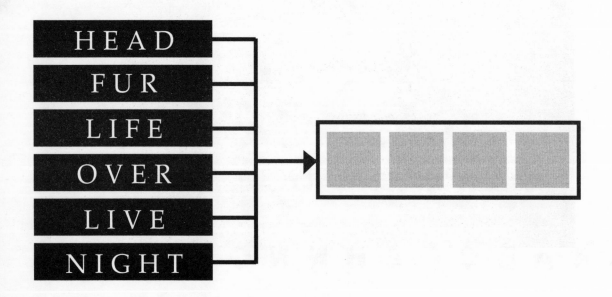

WORD PUZZLE 174

Which English word of four letters can be attached to the back of the words shown in the diagram to create six other words?

ANSWER 149

WORD PUZZLE 175

Select one letter from each of the segments.
When the correct letters have been found a word of eight letters
can be read clockwise. What is the word?

ANSWER 190

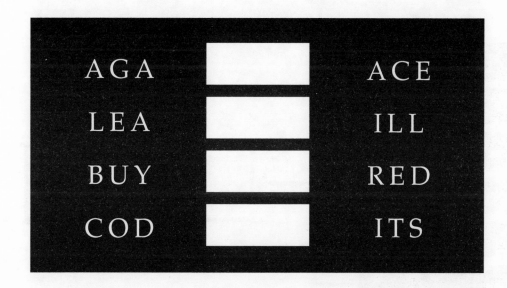

AGA		ACE
LEA		ILL
BUY		RED
COD		ITS

WORD PUZZLE 176

Place two letters in the empty space which, when added to the
words to the left and to the right, form other English words.
When this is completed another word can be read down.
What is the word?

ANSWER 138

WORD PUZZLE 177

Take the letters and arrange them correctly in the column under which they appear. Once this has been done the name of a novel and a movie will emerge. What is it?

ANSWER 180

W T F L
E I A I
T O C S
A O E T

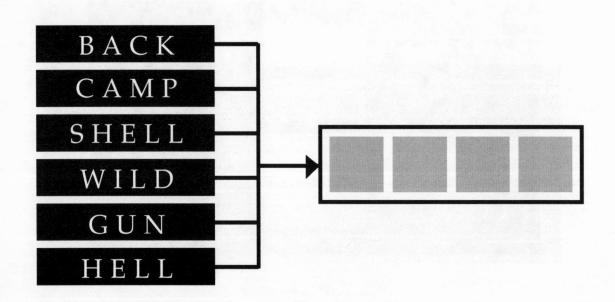

BACK
CAMP
SHELL
WILD
GUN
HELL

WORD PUZZLE 178

Which English word of four letters can be attached to the back of the words shown in the diagram to create six other words?

ANSWER 128

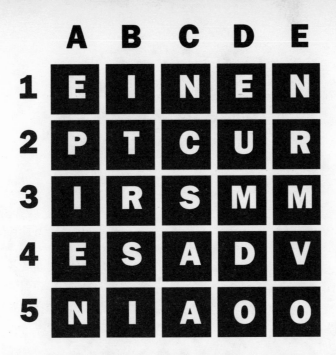

A B C D E

1 E I N E N
2 P T C U R
3 I R S M M
4 E S A D V
5 N I A O O

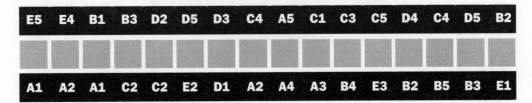

| E5 | E4 | B1 | B3 | D2 | D5 | D3 | C4 | A5 | C1 | C3 | C5 | D4 | C4 | D5 | B2 |
| A1 | A2 | A1 | C2 | C2 | E2 | D1 | A2 | A4 | A3 | B4 | E3 | B2 | B5 | B3 | E1 |

WORD PUZZLE 179

Select one of the two letters from the grid, in accordance with the reference shown, and place it in the word frame. When the correct letters have been chosen a sixteen-letter word can be read. What is the word?

ANSWER 170

WORD PUZZLE 180

Place an English word of THREE letters in the empty space. This word, when added to the end of the three words to the left and to the beginning of the three words to the right, will form six other words. What is the word?

ANSWER 118

WORD PUZZLE 181

Place one letter in the middle of this diagram. Four five-letter
words can now be rearranged from each straight line of letters.
What is the letter and what are the words?

ANSWER 159

WORD PUZZLE 182

Place an English word of THREE letters in the empty space. This
word, when added to the end of the three words to the left and to
the beginning of the three words to the right, will form six other
words. What is the word?

ANSWER 107

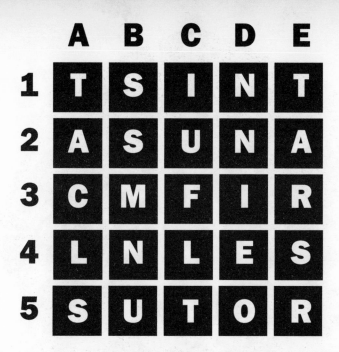

	A	B	C	D	E
1	T	S	I	N	T
2	A	S	U	N	A
3	C	M	F	I	R
4	L	N	L	E	S
5	S	U	T	O	R

D3	B4	B5	A1	A4	C2	D3	D4	D1	A2	A3	A4	D2	B2	D5	E3
C2	B1	A5	E2	E5	C4	B3	E1	C3	E1	E2	A1	C1	D2	C5	E4

WORD PUZZLE 183

Select one of the two letters from the grid, in accordance with the reference shown, and place it in the word frame. When the correct letters have been chosen a sixteen-letter word can be read.
What is the word?

ANSWER 200

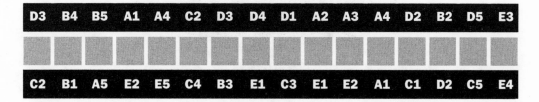

THE CAVE MAN SAT IN FRONT OF

THE FIRE, HOLDING A

PIECE OF • • • • • ON HIS KNEE, ON

WHICH WAS TO BE FOUND

SOME • • • • • FOOD.

WORD PUZZLE 184

Two words using the same letters in their construction can be used to replace the dots in this sentence. The sentence will then make sense. Each dot is one letter. What are the words?

ANSWER 148

WORD PUZZLE 185

Move from circle to touching circle collecting the letters of DIET.
Always start at the D.
How many different ways are there to do this?

ANSWER 189

SIREN	SWORD
DENIM	VASES
WIDOW	FOCUS
TIARA	LOTUS
MELON	RUPEE

WORD PUZZLE 186

Five of the words in the diagram are associated for some
reason. Find the words and then work out whether VISOR belongs
to the group.

ANSWER 137

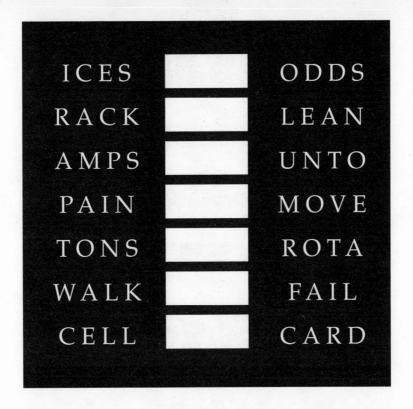

ICES   ODDS
RACK   LEAN
AMPS   UNTO
PAIN   MOVE
TONS   ROTA
WALK   FAIL
CELL   CARD

WORD PUZZLE 187

Change the first letter of each word to the left and the right. Two other English words must be formed. Place the letter used in the empty section. When this has been completed for all the words another English word can be read down. What is the word?

ANSWER 179

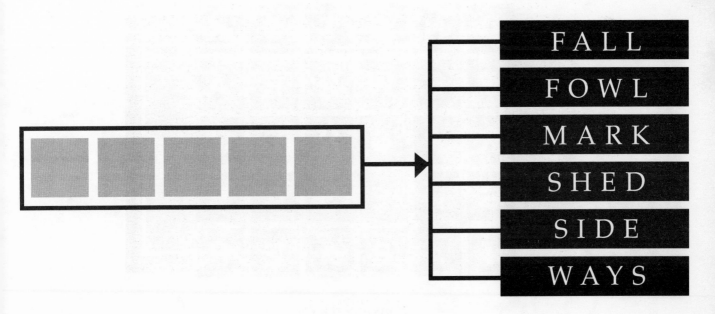

FALL
FOWL
MARK
SHED
SIDE
WAYS

WORD PUZZLE 188

Which English word of five letters can be attached to the front of the words shown in the diagram to create six other words?

ANSWER 127

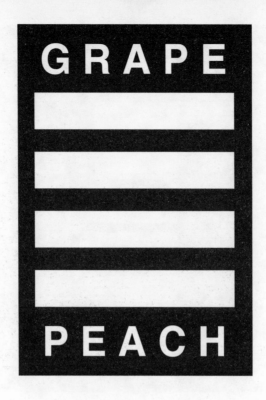

WORD PUZZLE 189

Complete the word ladder by changing one letter of each word
per step. The newly created word must be found in the dictionary.
What are the words to turn GRAPE to PEACH?

ANSWER 169

WORD PUZZLE 190

A proverb has been written in this diagram. Find the start letter
and move from square to touching square until you have found it.
What is it?

ANSWER 117

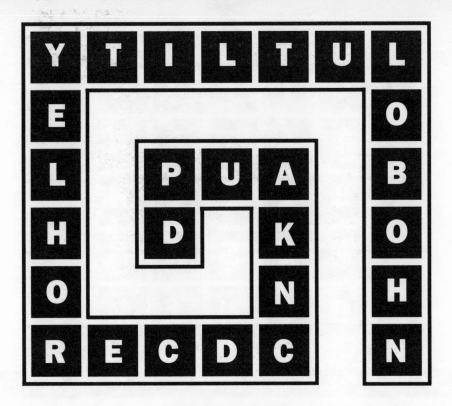

WORD PUZZLE 191

The names of three flowers are to be found in the diagram.
The letters of the names are in the order they normally appear.
What are the flowers?

ANSWER 158

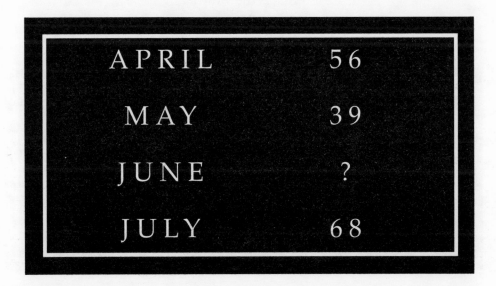

WORD PUZZLE 192

The diagram shows the sunshine hours in England for four
months . The numbers bear a relationship to the letters in the
words. What should replace the question mark?

ANSWER 106

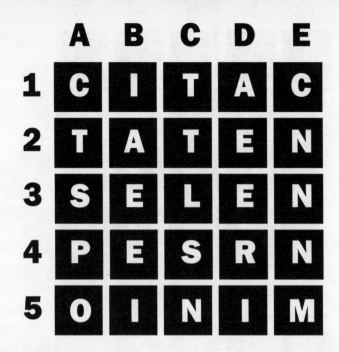

A B C D E

1 C I T A C
2 T A T E N
3 S E L E N
4 P E S R N
5 O I N I M

B5	E2	D1	E2	A3	A1	A5	B4	C2	B1	E1	B3	D2	A2	D5	B5
C1	D4	C1	D3	D4	A4	B2	E4	B4	E3	E3	B5	C5	C4	D1	C3

WORD PUZZLE 193

Select one of the two letters from the grid, in accordance with the reference shown, and place it in the word frame. When the correct letters have been chosen a sixteen-letter word can be read. What is the word?

ANSWER 199

THE WEIGHT LIFTER, ALTHOUGH

VERY • • • • • • •, FAILED IN HIS

ATTEMPT BECAUSE OF HIS

• • • • • • • APPROACH.

WORD PUZZLE 194

Two words using the same letters in their construction can be used to replace the dots in this sentence. The sentence will then make sense. Each dot is one letter. What are the words?

ANSWER 147

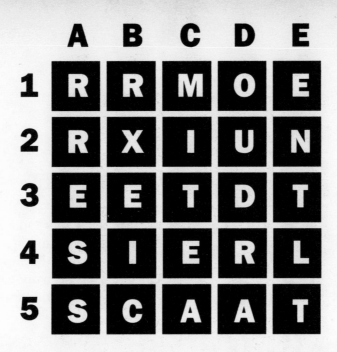

	A	B	C	D	E
1	R	R	M	O	E
2	R	X	I	U	N
3	E	E	T	D	T
4	S	I	E	R	L
5	S	C	A	A	T

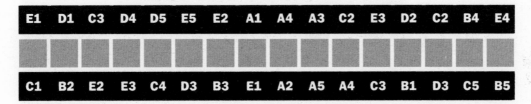

E1	D1	C3	D4	D5	E5	E2	A1	A4	A3	C2	E3	D2	C2	B4	E4
C1	B2	E2	E3	C4	D3	B3	E1	A2	A5	A4	C3	B1	D3	C5	B5

WORD PUZZLE 195

Select one of the two letters from the grid, in accordance with the
reference shown, and place it in the word frame. When the correct
letters have been chosen a sixteen-letter word can be read.
What is the word?

ANSWER 188

WORD PUZZLE 196

Make a circle out of these shapes.
When the correct circle has been found a word can be read
clockwise. What is the word?

ANSWER 136

R M S E

A O H O

F T E N

T H E E

WORD PUZZLE 197

Take the letters and arrange
them correctly in the column
under which they appear.
Once this has been done the name
of a movie will emerge.
What is it?

ANSWER 178

MAUVE   39

GREEN   26

CREAM   21

BLACK   ?

WORD PUZZLE 198

On this list of four colours the numbers bear a relationship to the
letters in the words. What should replace the question mark?

ANSWER 126

	A	B	C	D	E
1	P	S	T	S	T
2	Y	R	S	O	A
3	B	A	R	H	T
4	O	E	C	O	E
5	I	R	P	Y	H

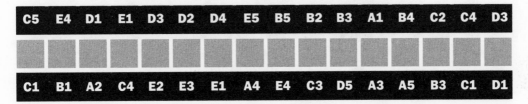

C5	E4	D1	E1	D3	D2	D4	E5	B5	B2	B3	A1	B4	C2	C4	D3
C1	B1	A2	C4	E2	E3	E1	A4	E4	C3	D5	A3	A5	B3	C1	D1

WORD PUZZLE 199

Select one of the two letters from the grid, in accordance with the
reference shown, and place it in the word frame. When the correct
letters have been chosen a sixteen-letter word can be read.
What is the word?

ANSWER 168

WORD PUZZLE 200

Two words using the same letters in their construction can be used
to replace the dots in this sentence. The sentence will then make
sense. Each dot is one letter. What are the words?

ANSWER 116

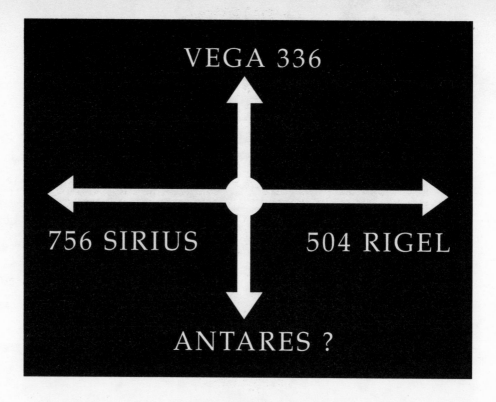

WORD PUZZLE 201

The diagram shows the light years to various stars. The numbers bear a relationship to the letters in the words. What should replace the question mark?

ANSWER 157

WORD PUZZLE 202

Place an English word of FOUR letters in the empty space. This word, when added to the end of the three words to the left and to the beginning of the three words to the right, will form six other words. What is the word?

ANSWER 105

WORD PUZZLE 203

Select one letter from each of the segments.
When the correct letters have been found a word of eight letters
can be read clockwise. What is the word?

ANSWER 198

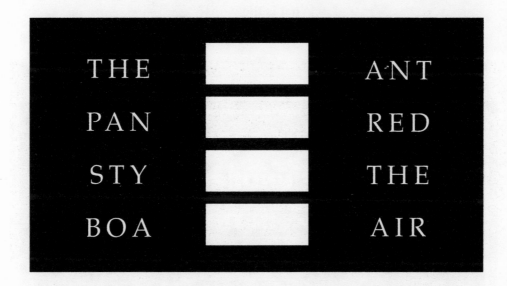

THE		ANT
PAN		RED
STY		THE
BOA		AIR

WORD PUZZLE 204

Place two letters in the empty space which, when added to the
words to the left and to the right, form other English words.
When this is completed another word can be read down.
What is the word?

ANSWER 146

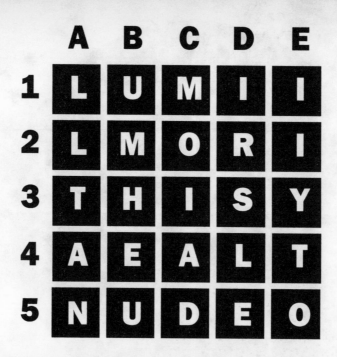

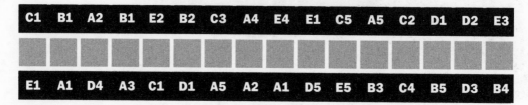

WORD PUZZLE 205

Select one of the two letters from the grid, in accordance with the reference shown, and place it in the word frame. When the correct letters have been chosen a sixteen-letter word can be read. What is the word?

ANSWER 187

WORD PUZZLE 206

Two words using the same letters in their construction can be used to replace the dots in this sentence. The sentence will then make sense. Each dot is one letter. What are the words?

ANSWER 135

Answers

1. Ohm, Stoop, Respond, and Chop.
2. Word, Oboe, Rode, and Deep.

3. Mow, Jewel, Blanket, and Down.
4. Back, Aeon, Cove, and Knew.

5. Ivy, Geese, Embrace, and Over.
6. Yard, Afar, Race, and Drew.

7. Fir, First, Firearm, and Fire.
8. Stop, Tame, Omen, and Pent.

9. Lid, Valid, Quality, and Will.
10. Tide, Idea, Deer, and Ears

11. Fire.
12. Rulers have no authority from God to do mischief. Jonathan Mayhew.
13. Bird.

14. The first casualty when war comes is truth. Hiram Johnson.
15. Well.
16. All animals are equal but some animals are more equal than others. George Orwell.
17. Like.
18. If you can't stand the heat keep out of the kitchen. President Harry Truman.
19. Den.
20. When you have to kill a man it costs nothing to be polite. Winston Churchill.
21. Rugged and Grudge.
22. Low.
23. Misunderstanding.
24. Buck.
25. 192. Each vowel is worth 6 and each consonant 8. The vowels are added together, as are the consonants. The totals are then multiplied.
26. Foot.
27. Brides and Debris.
28. Hand.
29. 21 ways.
30. Moon.
31. Tolerate.
32. Flute does not belong to the group. The five associated words are Decoy, Steam, Tulip, Abbey, and Hippo. The first two letters of each word are in alphabetical order.
33. Delegate.
34. 12 ways.
35. Imposter.

36. 8 ways.
37. Operator.
38. 9 ways.
39. Reunites.
40. Shell does not belong to the group. The linked words are Beast, Decor, Heron, Human, Pilaf, and Round. The first and last letter position in the alphabet totals 22.
41. Daffodil.
42. Nest.
43. Baseball.
44. Cast.
45. Woodbine.
46. Band.
47. Taxpayer.
48. Step.
49. Aardvark.
50. House.
51. Kindness.
52. B. To give Elbow, Orbit, Habit, and Noble.
53. Satinwood, Jacaranda, and Greengage.
54. A. To give Koala, Peace, Shade, and Whale.
55. Cannelloni, Macaroni, and Spaghetti.
56. J. To give Enjoy, Major, Rajah, and Dojos.
57. Champagne, Chocolate, and Orangeade.
58. H. To give Abhor, Ethic, Ochre, and Usher.
59. Harmonium, Accordion, Piano, and Tuba.

60. P. To give Capon, Hippo, Imply, and Paper.

61. Argentina, Australia, and Indonesia.

62. G. To give Angel, Anger, Cigar, and Logic.

63. 27. Each vowel is worth 2 and each consonant 3. The totals of the vowels and consonants are added.

64. Loon, Loop, Poop, Pomp, Pump.

65. 20. Each vowel is worth 4 and each consonant 2. The totals of the vowels and consonants are added.

66. Pong, Pang, Rang, Rant, Cant.

67. Summer Vacations.

68. Raver, Raves, Paves, Pares, Bares, Barks.

69. 57. Each letter is given its positional value in the alphabet and these are added together.

70. Shop, Shoe, Sloe, Floe, Flee, Free.

71. 108. Each vowel in the name is worth 10 and each consonant is worth 22. These are all added together to give the distance.

72. Sleds, Slews, Slows, Glows, Grows, Gross.

73. Benjamin Franklin.

74. Gesture.

75. Dances with Wolves.

76. Rainbow.

77. The Spy Who Loved Me.

78. Emerald.

79. Oscar Hammerstein.

80. Magenta.

81. Mary, Queen of Scots.

82. Crimson.

83. Nineteen.

84. 17 ways.

85. Journals.

86. Style belongs to the group. The linked words are Abyss, Buyer, Coypu, Idyll, and Mayor. All other words have Y as the third letter.

87. Historic.

88. Syrup does not belong to the group. The linked words are Cedar, Hedge, Medal, Sedan, and Wedge. All the words contain ED.

89. February.

90. Plant belongs to the group. The linked words are Burnt, Count, Event, Flint, and Giant. All the words end in NT.

91. Caffeine.

92. 5 ways

93. Unconstitutional.

94. 26 ways.

95. Disqualification.

96. 9 ways.

97. Characterization.

98. 22 ways.

99. Air-conditioning.

100. 14 ways.

101. Thanksgiving day.

102. 25 ways.

103. Acknowledgements.

104. Tango, Alien, Nines, Geese, and Onset

105. Port.

106. 50. The alphabetical values of the letters are added together.

107. Ten.

108. Sat, Bacon, Anchors, and Each.

109. Yeast, Eager, Agave, Seven, and Trend.

110. Cot, Attic, Cushion, and Both.

111. Facet, Above, Coven, Event, and Tents.

112. Ripens and Sniper.

113. Smile, Mania, Inset, Liege, and Eater.

114. Arm, Enter, Mansion, and Arts.

115. Cheer does belong to the group. The associated words are Jetty, Comma, Annoy, Caddy, and Steel. Each have double letters.

116. Itself and Stifle.

117. Absence makes the heart grow fonder.

118. Eye.

119. Every man meets his Waterloo at last. Wendell Phillips.

120. Umpire and Impure.

121. Die my dear doctor thats the last thing I shall do. Lord Palmerston

122. Her.

123. One more such victory and we are lost. Pyrrhus.

124. End.

125. 6 ways.

126. 14. The alphabetical values of the first, third and fifth letters are added together.

127. Water.

128. Fire.

129. Flat.

130. Dance, Acorn, Nomad, Crave, and Ended.

131. Met, Amaze, Chamber, and Team.

132. Had, Blink, Academy, and Raid.

133. Ram.

134. Fantasy.

135. Writhes and Withers.

136. Macaroni.

137. Visor belongs to the group. The associated words are Vases, Denim, Widow, Focus, and Lotus. In each word the vowels appear in alphabetical order.

138. Pestered.

139. Globe does not belong to the group. The associated words are Hymns, Light, Ankle, Films, Index, and Pasta. Each word contains two letters next to each other which appear consecutively in the alphabet.

140. Deadline.

141. Widow belongs to the group. The associated words are Dread, Kiosk, Loyal, Arena, and Comic. Each word begins and ends with the same letter.

142. Teaspoon.

143. Cafes belongs to the group. The associated words are Babes, Games, Cakes, Paper, and Tales. Each have A and E as their second and fourth letter.

144. Gathered.

145. Comment is free but facts are sacred. C.P. Scott.

146. Medalist.

147. Muscly and Clumsy.

148. Slate and Stale.

149. Long.

150. Jealousy.

151. Red.

152. Suitcase.

153. Boy.

154. Gardener.

155. Man.

156. Sun.

157. 1008. Each consonant is worth 7 and each vowel 12. The consonant total is multiplied by the vowel total.

158. Hollyhock, Buttercup, and Dandelion.

159. S. To give Basic, Eased, Haste (or Heats), and Music.

160. Butterfly, Centipede, and Cockroach.

161. E. To give Agent, Bleak, Enemy, and Query.

162. Decorator, Policeman, and Architect.

163. V. To give Civic, Devil, Haven, and Lever.

164. Coriander, Asparagus, and Artichoke.

165. K. To give Joked, Maker, Taken, and Yokel.

166. Wolverine , Armadillo, and Porcupine.

167. 16 ways.

168. Psychotherapists.

169. Grace, Glace, Place, Peace.

170. Overcompensation.

171. Sort, Soot, Shot, Shop.

172. Responsibilities.

173. Prop, Poop, Pool, Poll, Pall.

174. 114. A is given the value 6, B is given 7 and so forth. The letter values in each word are added together.

175. Stare, Stars, Stays, Slays.

176. 57. The first and last letters are given the value of their position in the alphabet. These are then added together.

177. 5 ways.

178. The Name of the Rose.

179. Ability.

180. A Tale of Two Cities.

181. Badgers.

182. Star Trek the Movie.

183. Calypso.

184. George Washington.

185. Delight.

186. Winston Churchill.

187. Multimillionaire.

188. Extraterrestrial.

189. 11 ways.

190. Macaroon

191. 18 ways.

192. Ultimate.

193. 16 ways.

194. Horsefly.

195. 21 ways.

196. Puzzlers.

197. Glaze, Glare, Glary.

198. Radiance.

199. Intercontinental.

200. Instrumentalists

201. 10 ways.

202. Enthusiastically.

203. Crated and Carted.

204. Conservationists.

205. 8 ways.

206. Subconsciousness.

YOUR PUZZLE NOTES

YOUR PUZZLE NOTES

YOUR PUZZLE NOTES

YOUR PUZZLE NOTES

YOUR PUZZLE NOTES

1
2 6
2 6
9
4 6
8